COMMISSIONS AT
RISK

A Real Estate Professional's Guide to Beating *Online* Competition

Danielle Babb, PhD, MBA

KAPLAN) PUBLISHING

President, Kaplan Publishing: Roy Lipner
Vice President and Publisher: Maureen McMahon
Acquisitions Editor: Victoria Smith
Production Editor: Michael Hankes
Typesetter: Ellen Gurak
Cover Designer: Gail Chandler

Published by Kaplan Publishing,
a division of Kaplan, Inc.

Printed in the United States of America

06 07 08 10 9 8 7 6 5 4 3 2 1

Library of Congress Cataloging-in-Publication Data

Commissions at risk : a real estate professional's guide to beating online competition / by Danielle Babb.
    p. cm.
Includes bibliographical references.
ISBN-13: 978-1-4195-9323-9
ISBN-10: 1-4195-9323-4
1. Real estate business—Computer network resources. 2. Real estate business—Technological innovations. I. Title.

HD1380.6.B32 2006
333.3068–dc22

2006025568

Kaplan Publishing books are available at special quantity discounts to use for sales promotions, employee premiums, or educational purposes. Please call our Special Sales Department to order or for more information at 800-621-9621, ext. 4444; e-mail *kaplanpubsales@kaplan.com;* or write to Kaplan Publishing, 30 South Wacker Drive, Suite 2500, Chicago, IL 60606-7481.

Contents

After studying and working in the technology field for more than 13 years and earning a doctorate with a technology management emphasis, I was introduced to the exciting world of investing in real estate by a good friend. It seemed a natural fit because many of my years spent as an IT director were with real estate companies of various types: commercial, residential, and property management. Within months, I quickly learned that my skills as an IT professional could be put to good use at real estate companies trying to keep up with constantly changing technology, increasing demands from clients, and a loss of the proprietary information that made them money. My bachelor's, master's, and doctoral students began studying the impact of technology on service industries, and real estate repeatedly surfaced.

I began consulting with real estate companies to improve their technology and help them gain a competitive edge—or at least catch up. What I quickly learned was that the Internet was permanently changing the real estate industry as we know it today, and that those who were unable to keep up would quickly see their profits drop or be put out of business altogether. What was most bothersome was that real estate agents didn't seem to realize this. They saw technology as an enhancement rather than a threat—Web-enabling a business that was about to undergo rapid and dramatic transformation. My consulting business quickly changed to helping real estate companies prepare for this shift that would create a Web-based business rather than a Web-enabled business.

This realization of a paradigm change coincided with a technology conference I was asked to present at, where I chose to discuss an aspect of information technology and business coupled with research—the obvious answer was real estate. In preparing for the presentation, I conducted primary research along with the help of two great friends and colleagues to find out what real estate professionals think of the changes, and whether they find them threatening or appealing. Most were using the Internet to enhance communications, unaware of the change in the marketplace that was rapidly occurring and the movement toward transaction-based systems that would remove the need for hand-holding through the process. In fact, most of the applications that need to be developed for successful transformation have *already been developed,* but many real estate professionals are blissfully unaware of this. The slow process of integration is the only thing that has held back the progress; however, the integration is nearly complete.

It became quickly apparent that real estate professionals were unaware that the technological shift to a Web-based business with low-cost providers was about to occur. Still focusing on their old ways of doing business, they are risking their future success. Thus began the motivation for creating a book, one that would both educate consumers on the tools available to them today and how to work within the Web-based framework to make transactions efficient and quick, and a solution for real estate professionals who want to build a business that can survive the dramatic shift occurring, thanks almost entirely to the availability of technology to mimic complicated systems. In the process, the middleman has been eliminated in many industries; real estate is next. More interestingly, I began to find ways that real estate professionals can survive, even thrive, in a marketplace that will create an environment by which these professionals are competing with the very technology they embraced not long ago.

This author has a rather unique and educated opinion on this topic: Real estate professionals must successfully prepare themselves for tomorrow's Web-based systems, not Web-enabled systems, which will rapidly integrate and replace their traditional ways of doing business if they wish to continue working in real estate. The consumer has an incredible power of information never seen before in real estate, leveling the playing field, lowering costs, and creating a dynamic and efficient environment for those wishing to buy or sell real estate. Therefore it's imperative that real estate professionals make rapid changes in their business, strategize for the future, and decide where and how they want to position themselves before it's too late.

My name is Danielle Babb; I have a PhD in organization and management with a technology emphasis, an MBA with a technology emphasis, and a bachelor's degree in business. I am an expert in the use of technology, business, and real estate. I teach courses at all levels on this topic, and present nationally and internationally on the topic of using technology to turn service industries into commodities. It is my intention that every reader of this book become more enlightened about the reality of the Internet and what it will (and won't) do for the real estate business, and how to become successful in the age of Web-based transaction systems. Real estate professionals will become acutely aware of the tools available to their clients, the consumers, and will understand what it is they will be competing with in the very near future. Not only will my readers become educated on the facts, they will be given tools to equip themselves for future success. The change has just begun. Comments to the author are always welcome. The book's Web site is *www.commissions-at-risk.com.*

A threat is growing in the real estate business, skirting along nicely under the radar of many real estate professionals. The technology being developed and already deployed is designed specifically to compete with you. No one disputes that technology is profoundly impacting every area of business and just about every market known to man. Everywhere we turn, "brick and mortar" is turning to "click and mortar," or just "click," depending on the industry. In many market sectors, the middleman is being eliminated entirely or the role of a middleman is being drastically changed. Some technologists and consumers see real estate professionals as the middlemen to otherwise low-cost, successful transactions. The real estate industry has been slowly impacted by technology because transactions are relatively complicated, with many people "touching" the transaction before it is considered complete. The more complicated the transaction, the more difficult it is to mimic online. The code has been cracked and companies are creating systems that will allow buyers and sellers to exchange goods—homes—directly online. Already low-cost and flat-fee brokers have created extreme competition in some hot markets. The detrimental impact to your business is imminent. Technology is creeping up in both the residential and investment real estate sectors. *The world as you know it is about to change.*

As with any technological revolution, some markets are hit more rapidly than others. Consumers are now able to search for homes using a Multiple Listing Service (MLS). They can list their homes online and post their home listings in the MLS. They can secure a low-cost or flat-fee broker to handle the paperwork entirely online. They can create their own virtual tours, they can add photos to their listings, and they can even place lockboxes on their homes and put the codes in the MLS—just like real estate agents do. Technology about to be released will take this many steps further, completing entire transactions online, including e-signing and wiring money—all without paying 5 percent to 6 percent commission. Just as the real estate agent will be impacted, so will others in the industry, including mortgage brokers, bankers and lenders, and those offering other ancillary services.

Many of us have used Amazon and have seen the amazing power of pricing tools that instantly compare prices of a product at hundreds of Web sites, including shipping and tax. These types of sites have made many products commodities and have put many businesses out of commission. But they've also done something else—they have created entirely new e-businesses that are extremely successful and wildly popular. Many have competed with successful e-commerce companies and transformed their brick-and-mortar stores. A number of entrepreneurs have created new businesses that have been experiencing amazing returns. As real estate professionals, you must not only be prepared to compete against online systems that have already emerged, but you must prepare yourself for what is about to be the most drastic change we've seen in real estate in most of our lifetimes. You need to know what technology is out there and what consumers are using, and you need to be educated about opportunities for advancements in your field that will allow you to compete with the threats you face.

No doubt, online tools have brought many of you clients because they search for a home online, find one, and then contact a professional. This is true whether it is for a mortgage or for actually buying a home. Soon, however, the clients won't need an intervening third party; they will be able to complete their entire transactions online. Already they are able to list their homes on the MLS, a system real estate professionals once had exclusive access to. *Many seminars and books are available for real estate professionals on how to "catch up" with today's technology, but none,*

absolutely none, talk about how to prepare for what is about to happen—
until now.

Unfortunately, a lot of emphasis has been placed on bringing the real estate profession into the technology age. Many of you may have Web-based systems that even include MLS searching. Mortgage experts may have rates and calculators on their sites. But the new wave of technology goes far beyond this. The Web-based world is changing at a pace more rapid than we've seen in the past. Consumers are more savvy today than they were just three years ago. The everyday investor or residential homeseller will benefit tremendously, and numerous tools are being developed that appear to be sliding under the radar of even the most savvy real estate professionals. Even academics who are studying the transition have not made much headway with reporting the paradigm shift we're seeing in the markets and the technology we know is about to be sent into cyberspace. Low-cost and flat-fee brokers are enhancing the process of buying and selling online, and they are doing it cheaply, adding to your competition. New partnerships are sure to create technology that could wreak havoc on your career.

Don't underestimate the tremendous impact technological changes and a shift in supply will have on your business, potentially eliminating your job entirely or, at the very least, dramatically reducing your commissions as you struggle to compete with low-cost or flat-fee brokers who still add value to the process. This need not be the case; you can learn how other industries and markets have been impacted and make adjustments today to accommodate for what is about to occur. If you don't, you will find yourself in the same position that many in the travel industry have—looking for a new career or living on a portion of your previous income. Consumers and investors are quickly learning about the tools available to them; even local news programs are featuring new tools for real estate searching, purchasing, and analysis. Even though the real estate professional has largely ignored the impact, it can be ignored no longer. The marketplace is shifting from Web enabled to Web based, and this will have a significant impact on real estate professionals and consumers.

Throughout this book, you will be taken on a journey through the use of technology today, the capabilities of what is available, the ways in which you will need to remove the walls you've built around your information, and how to position yourself to compete in a marketplace where strictly having information is no longer an asset. Technology is known to level playing fields, and it's doing it right before your very eyes. By reading this book, you'll understand the Internet's greatest threat to your business and what to do to compete with it. You'll understand how the traditional ways of protecting your business do not work in a market where information that used to be private is readily available to the public. You will understand how the rapid integration of technology will change the way you've done everything in the past. You must understand this if you wish to successfully navigate the incredible changes occurring in technology that will impact the industry and your livelihood.

For the sake of discussion in this book, real estate professionals are defined as those related to or involved in the real estate transaction. This includes the real estate agent, mortgage broker, real estate broker, mortgage lender, appraisers, title and insurance companies, you name it. Anyone affected by the ups and downs of the real estate market will be affected by the technology coming your way.

You'll discover the reasons why so many of you will need to find a new niche to compete in a changing market, or risk losing your job. Most important, you will learn new ways to market yourself and find your way through an ever-changing market where the Internet is key and the buyers and sellers have more control than ever over the process. You will become aware of what your own colleagues are saying through firsthand analysis and research, and learn which tools and techniques you may use to find a niche for your services while still using your expertise. Navigating the technological minefield will prove difficult but worthwhile to those who are successful. A key to successfully surviving the coming changes is to be aware of what they are and then modify your business strategy accordingly. Just as consumers will benefit from the vast array of tools available to them whether they choose to complete transactions online or choose to use more traditional means to acquire property, this is certainly not in your best interest as a real estate professional. However, there are ways you can modify your business to even benefit from the changes.

The Internet is in what we technologists call "Web v. 2," which in plain English means the second version. This new set of Web-based tools transforms services into commodities; the first wave focused primarily on products that were easier to sell online. But the Internet is also doing something that is great for your business—it is literally creating markets. This may be an opening for you to position yourself for future work and to find your niche. In this book, I will explore ways in which the Internet is aiding investors in literally creating markets, and what the potential impact to those markets will be over the long term. Many questions will be asked and answers discovered, including the impact of the Internet on the "bubble" that so many experts have been saying will burst—yet hasn't in many areas. How does this compare to recent history or to the stock market? What role is the Internet playing in cushioning the supposed bubble that exists in the market today? Why aren't more of you paying attention to the tools that are rapidly threatening the way you do business? These topics and more will be explored in-depth in the chapters that follow. By the end of this book, you will be empowered to change your real estate business and to not only adapt to technology, but to beat your online competition.

1

TECHNOLOGY AND
REAL ESTATE

An incredible link exists between technology and real estate, beyond using systems for forms and listings. Information technology (IT) is hot on the agenda at real estate conferences, yet the incredible threat that the Internet poses to real estate professionals is often overlooked. If you want to be successful, you must acknowledge the risk caused by the explosion of Internet technologies and make changes before it forces them on you. These changes will affect nearly 4 million real estate professionals, creating a tremendous impact on an incredible marketplace.

The technology needed to transform real estate to a Web-based business is already being integrated today with systems completely capable of replacing traditional real estate models. Now technologists can mimic complicated processes online with a series of computer systems, so the need for many real estate professionals is diminishing because consumers are less willing to pay high-priced commissions for something they can do online themselves in a matter of a couple of hours. Everything from listing a home, creating a virtual tour, adding pictures, putting a lockbox on a home, finding buyers, showing the home, and even e-closing and e-signing can be handled electronically. As companies integrate these systems, consumers will see the great opportunity they have to save money when selling their home. Low-cost and flat-fee brokers and real estate companies are already taking over many market segments and moving in on the traditional real estate professional's territory. These low-cost brokers and flat-fee agents make their online homebuying and homeselling as easy and seamless as possible because it attracts and retains clients.

Real estate has long been a person-to-person industry, relying largely on personal relationships and trust. That relationship, however, is now being impacted by Internet-savvy consumers who are cashing in on pricey home sales. The more expensive the home, the more they must pay in commissions. People are less willing to do that with the alternatives presented—and these alternatives are online. As with any good or service, as the quantity of the available service goes up, the price goes down. This means lower commissions; something that the online brokers and flat-fee companies have already adjusted for but traditional real estate professionals have yet to manage. Using Web-based systems is fast becoming a viable alternative to the real estate agent or mortgage broker—and to the many other service professionals who provide third-party services for real estate transactions such as escrow and title companies, mortgage lenders, appraisers, and inspectors. In the future, the "middleman"—anyone involved in the process who can be replaced by an automated system—will be largely driven out of the market, leaving behind a series of Web-based systems to handle much of the processing and transaction-based work that real estate professionals have previously handled.

The real estate industry relies heavily on access to a large amount of information that until recently was proprietary and required consumers to work with professionals to obtain. Real estate agents connect buyers and sellers while mortgage brokers connect borrowers with lenders. Both professionals offer services that until a short time ago were very hard to duplicate in their entirety online. In other industries, we have seen a much earlier shift to technology because the process of the service was not so difficult or complicated as real estate is. However, processes and transactions can now be replicated with technology, and soon services will be available that enable the buyer and seller to complete every aspect of a transaction online, including purchasing, contracts, negotiations, lending, and closing. Much as we've seen in other service industries that were less difficult to replicate (such as travel and high-end retail), real estate is about to undergo a complete transformation that will forever change the market and need for real estate professionals. The sooner you understand the impact that Web-based transactions will have on your business, the sooner you can prepare yourself for the years to come.

TRANSACTION-BASED RISKS

Because real estate and lending are both transaction-based systems, these relationships and processes will more likely be replaced with online services. While the industry has been aware of these capabilities, only bits and pieces of the process have been automated. Soon, however, packages will be released that will automate the entire transaction from "cradle to grave." At that point, what will you offer to your clients that won't be available online? It's not enough to answer that question by saying "a personal touch"—many consumers don't want it for the price.

Information technology has always taken an underlying role—obtaining loan approvals but not completing the transaction, for example. The advent of new technology to be released in the next two years, such as e-signing and purely online loans along with standards created for these transactions to ensure every system can talk to other systems, will allow information technology to take an active role and eventually replace many brokers, agents, and other professionals in the industry such as appraisers and title companies.

Anytime there is an increased supply of a service, the price for that service drops. As Web-based services are rapidly deployed, the industry will be saturated with inexpensive services—as much as 90 percent lower—and only individuals who are ready for the transition will be able to compete.

As a real estate professional, you are keenly aware of your role and most likely the history of your industry. You must understand, however, how technology is changing the way people do business. As individuals become increasingly comfortable with buying and selling property using online services (and this is particularly true for younger generations who have grown up with computers), the need for real estate professionals will diminish, and you will need to equip yourself with the tools to compete in this changing industry. This has happened in other industries: The once-privy professional is replaced by information-driven Web sites, creating entire groups of professionals who no longer can compete with the convenience and inexpensive services that their new online competition provides. These professionals, especially those in the travel industry, have been so affected that they had to leave the industry because they did not prepare their businesses for the transition.

WORRIED OR NOT?

Many real estate professionals are worried, whether they admit it publicly or not. While many are still unaware of the imposing force that is going to affect their businesses, other professionals have embraced the wonderful changes technology has brought to their lives, particularly in a fast-paced market where interest rates have been low and real estate was considered as a replacement for stock investing. Technology has provided professionals with fast access to their clients, lots of leads without doing the old-fashioned legwork, online multiple listing service (MLS) listings, virtual tours, client management, and a wonderful marketing tool—the Web site! What you need to understand, however, is that the future of technology is **not** *Web enablement but Web based,* and this creates a new ballgame for you.

When we look at the drastic changes that have occurred in similar industries, such as travel, where an agent handles the details of a transaction, we can see what is about to happen in real estate. Many signs indicate that the transition has already begun, and now the technologies that have helped you increase your business will very soon be your biggest competitor. This can be a good or a bad thing, depending on your level of preparedness.

THE TRENDS IN THE MEDIA

A look at publications, even local newspapers, reveals the trend toward information technology hitting the mainstream in real estate. The *Los Gatos Weekly-Times* on October 12, 2005, covered the California Association of REALTORS Centennial Expo (which included delegates from the Silicon Valley Association of REALTORS) in San Diego, California, and reported on developments in the real estate industry. During the conference, leaders in real estate discussed trends and, in particular, the results of a technology survey.

According to the report, technology has become such an integral part of real estate transactions today that an entire day at the conference was devoted to training. Called "Tech Tuesday," the day started with a panel discussion of the role of technology in the real estate industry. This revealed a rapid adaptation to existing technology, but not necessarily an outlook on what the future holds and how to position the business for growth in a constantly changing culture that is heavily reliant on the Internet. According to the newspaper, a survey taken in 2005 revealed that 90 percent of real estate agents have high-speed Internet access at home, an increase from 82 percent in 2004 and 71 percent in 2003. For 46 percent of agents, electronic mail, or e-mail, is their primary form of communication with clients. Some 31 percent of agents noted that their most important technology upgrades in 2005 were handheld devices that allowed them to retrieve e-mail remotely. Real estate professionals are rapidly purchasing products to get them up to speed today, but they are ignoring the reality of tomorrow.

In the survey, the newspaper also noted that 60 percent of agents post listings to their own Web sites and 67 percent view the Internet as extremely or very important in marketing and promoting their sales. This survey revealed that 33 percent of business comes from the Internet. My own research as reported in subsequent chapters reveals an even greater number. Again, this indicates a focus on catching up with the technology available today but not a look at what the future will bring.

Now let's take a look at how the industry has changed in a little over ten years. In 1995, only 2 percent of homebuyers used the Internet as a source of information. In 1997, this rose to 18 percent. In 1999, this figure more than doubled to 37 percent. In 2003, the number rose to more than 40 percent. We can easily see the trend has continued in today's marketplace. The Internet offers a tremendous value for homebuyers and investors who are looking to find, purchase, and rent property with ease and little hassle.

Technology has forever changed the way real estate is discovered, researched, purchased, and sold for the consumer; it has all but handed new clients to real estate professionals. But the best has yet to come—for the consumer. The Internet will soon put the buyer and seller in ultimate control, if they choose, of the entire process, leading to incredible savings for both parties but eliminating the need for professional involvement to complete the transaction. Your role now as a real estate professional is to revamp the industry and your own personal business to compete in this new marketplace. While real estate professionals used to be the keepers of once-proprietary information, Web services now offer this information to the buyer and the seller. Without having sole access to this information, you will no longer be an essential part to this transaction. The key with the new technology being deployed is that you cannot embrace it as a real estate professional, because it is designed inherently to *compete with you!* Therefore you must adopt a new strategy and face it head-on.

WEB COMPANIES WANT YOUR CLIENTS AND YOUR MONEY

In the process of developing and creating Web sites to boost your own revenues, you have essentially led the way for creative entrepreneurs to create systems that will rapidly be your biggest nemesis, transactions systems that will simplify and streamline many of the things you do for your clients.

If you, as a real estate professional, try to stay one step ahead of the game and focus on what is about to happen rather than playing catch-up to what has already occurred, you will stand a greater chance of weathering the impending storm. Of course, first you need to create some of the basics—a Web site and a reliable e-mail system if you don't have one already. The technology you are used to made your life easier, but the new wave of technology won't make your life easier or bring you new leads. The hottest real estate technology companies are not focusing on how to make your life better, but how to replace you entirely.

The Internet has already decreased the demand for real estate professionals in the United States, as more and more information than ever is available to consumers online. Many of the details, though, still need to be handled by individuals, and that is where many real estate professionals have actually enjoyed increasing revenues as a result. Elements such as comparative analyses (comps), bank mortgage rates, access to appraisers and home inspectors, and escrow companies can now be researched and found online. Once an investor buys a property, he or she can secure a property manager in a matter of hours, all with competing quotes and online contracts. Just a couple of years ago, information was safely guarded by professionals who then charged for this data in the form of "applied expertise." Buyers and sellers are finding it easier than ever to sell by owner and skip the fees of an agent entirely, while virtually managing the process from their desktops. Low-cost brokers are changing the business by providing full service by salaried real estate professionals at half the commission rates. Many experts didn't predict this trend to impact banking, travel, or any other service industry, yet it has. Real estate is next.

OLD STRATEGIES, NEW TECHNOLOGIES

Real estate professionals are keenly aware of many of the strategies they or their organizations use to keep business coming and sustain their incomes. As in other businesses, real estate professionals use personal relationships to create pressure to use their services, whether this is in the consumers' best interest or not. Your clients have probably received calendars, notepads, magnets, even garage sale materials from you in an effort to keep your name on the tip of their tongue should they decide to buy or sell a home. These have been excellent marketing tools, and the real estate profession should be commended for the creative ways they have become experts in entire markets. These constant reminders worked when the profession existed as a service to those who were overwhelmed by the process and rules of buying and selling real estate. As a professional, you must understand that the same marketing techniques will not work with the Web tools about to be deployed, or even with those of low-cost brokers who already exist online. The need for a professional to match a buyer and seller is decreasing at a steady rate; after all, buyers are purchasing homes, not relationships with sellers. With interest rates at historically low levels and a quarter of all home purchases made by investors, there is little engagement of a personal nature. Because of the convenience and accessibility, many buyers today come to agents with homes already in mind that they found on the Internet. Likewise, they are coming with prequalified loans from direct-to-lender Web sites. With these two steps already simplified, what if the buyer could look at the home without the agent, complete the entire transaction online, and move in when escrow closes—all without touching the hands of an agent, broker, appraiser, or traditional title or escrow company? Will it happen?

Absolutely! Tens of thousands of technology experts are hot on the trail.

So what's in it for the seller besides greater efficiency? Lower costs. As home prices go up, 5 percent or 6 percent becomes a greater dollar amount paid in commissions to the agent than ever before. A home worth $500,000 just five years ago could be sold by an agent for $25,000 to $30,000. Today that same home, worth $1,000,000, will require the sellers to pay commissions of $50,000 to $60,000—something many sellers are just unwilling to do. The seller's costs no doubt will be reduced, which often results in a better price for the buyer for many sellers factor the real estate agents' commission into the selling price. The mortgage broker has no margins left and is incapable of selling a loan with an inflated interest rate or high-yield spreads. The entire process happens faster with less hassle than if you were directly involved and managing the transaction—at least the way the industry is structured today.

This is what you have to compete with. In fact, many consumer advocates would welcome a change that would mean you, as a real estate professional, are no longer employed or frequently used by most consumers because many consumers feel that the work and effort required is not worth tens of thousand of dollars. Many would rather look up some information online, price their home accordingly, and sit during open houses on the weekends. In fact, many sites are devoted to helping sellers make their home "ready for sale," including tips from removing odors to storing clutter. Whether you agree with this opinion or not, you must pay attention to it because your clients are, and this sentiment, coupled with Web systems, may take away your business.

As an agent or broker, you must modify your business practice and create a place for yourself in the new marketplace. Consumers will be extremely aware of the tools available to them, and you need to be familiar with these tools that can potentially remove you from the process. Consumers, by choosing low-cost Web-based systems, will be making a choice and setting the tone for your profession. Rather than sitting back and waiting for this to occur, you must take control of your business and position your work for the new market. This book is the first step toward helping you do that.

e-BUSINESS AND REAL ESTATE

BusinessWeek magazine conducts an e-business report on markets impacted by technology. Among them, it reported on the real estate market and the transformation created by the Web. Fascinating statistics revealed and validated that consumers are often bringing the homes they're interested in right to your doorstep, making your job very easy. Soon, they'll find the same home and buy it online—without you.

The survey found that as of June 2004, 70 percent of homebuyers shopped online before signing any deals, which was up from 41 percent in 2001. This growth trend is incredible and can be frightening if you're not prepared. Online real estate middlemen collected less than 1 percent of $60 billion in real estate commission fees paid in 2003, but that is expected to increase to 4 percent by 2007 (Real Trends). While this doesn't seem like a large number at first glance, other factors are not considered, such as the ability to secure a direct-to-lender loan and purchase or sell a property online without human intervention that may often slow down a transaction. If this trend continues, the middleman role many professionals currently play may be going by the wayside with Internet tools handling most of the transactions. This doesn't mean there will be no market or business for your work, but it does mean that you need to rethink and strategize on how you'll fit into this new market.

THE POWER OF SELF-SERVICE

As agents know, individuals are more often turning to for-sale-by-owner (FSBO) do-it-yourself sites and low-cost/flat-fee agents or brokers to market and sell their homes. To counter this measure, many real estate organizations market their services as value-added and necessary for successful and stress-free transactions. Numerous commercials focus on how buyers need protection, sellers need good and rapid service, and the entire process is "so complicated"—an unfounded fear tactic used to sell real estate services. Please don't rely on this to save your business! Brokers scare consumers or tell them tales of providing the "best loan" to them, all while increasing their interest rate to get better commissions or charging enormous fees. The value isn't there for either profession given today's technological standard, and quite soon most Internet-savvy consumers will be aware of this. You will need to be one step ahead of this game if you are going to survive.

If the buyers and sellers, for $40, could download all the online forms they need, submit them to an escrow company online, coordinate their appraisals and loans, and close the process all by clicking the mouse and electronically wiring money, wouldn't they? This certainly will not provide an enhancement to the way real estate professionals do business, but rather a replacement. Technology in real estate has a goal, and that is to take your money and your clients. Many new systems will allow the process to be completed entirely online, including e-notary and e-signing.

WHERE'S THE VALUE?

Some real estate brokers, agents, or companies may live up to the promise of making life easier and relieving the worry and stress from the average homeseller or homebuyer, but there are Internet companies that also help walk a consumer through this process. How much better is working with an individual in person versus an individual online? As Internet-friendly Web sites emerge and younger generations, already completely comfortable and familiar with online transactions, become homebuyers and homesellers, companies will find it more difficult to live up to a value-added promise. At what price is the "service" of hand-

holding by a person rather than someone behind an e-mail address valuable? Many consumers, at 5 percent to 6 percent
commission rates, are asking that very question. This 5 percent to
6 percent on a bag of groceries isn't a lot for some families, but 5
percent to 6 percent of the sales price of a home means thousands
of dollars lost in the sale of a piece of real estate. For baby
boomers, it means retirement money. For young families, it
means lower-priced homes they can purchase when they move. As
the markets soften a bit, many consumers may be unwilling to pay
fees they could otherwise pocket themselves. You need to be
aware of this to know how to compete with it.

PATH TO COMMODITY

As a result of the vast amount of information and tools available online to consumers, the Internet is making many of the
hands that touch these transactions commodities, such as long-
distance service or travel. Unless you're traveling somewhere your
travel agent has been to hundreds of times and you want his or her
professional advice, what value does going and sitting at a travel
agent's desk bring to you? In fact, many of you reading this book
probably book your travel using one of the many travel sites designed to make it cheaper and easier to move about the world. Is
a special deal or a great package price going to lure you to an
agent who you have to go visit, sit down with, and take hours to
do book? Perhaps in the past, but probably not today when compared with the tremendous value that online travel-booking companies offer because of their low cost and streamlined
efficiencies, not to mention their deals with major hotel chains,
rental car agencies, and airlines.

The travel industry is such an interesting paradigm to real estate that it's worth noting that some hotels are so worried about
online companies that they've forbidden their franchisees to partner with Internet organizations or risk losing their license or deal
with steep fines. In fact, once the airlines were able to offer Web

sites to issue electronic tickets, airlines sold them directly to the public, closing down sales offices in major cities and capping travel agents' commission to as low as $50 per ticket. In many cases, agents were unable to make a living doing what they did for years.

So what is the attraction of continuing to do business with an agent? Apparently not much, given the statistics of the travel industry. It's all the same, so go with the cheapest. Personal research confirms this, which is also discussed in later chapters in greater detail, with many correlations between travel and real estate drawn clearly for your review.

REAL ESTATE'S INHERENT PROTECTION

Real estate has thus far been somewhat protected from any drastic changes because the process touches so many hands and businesses and is so complicated for technologists to mimic that it's been difficult for the IT folks to create a system that does what you do. This is because of a number of factors: the perceived difficulty in completing transactions, agents' unwillingness to work with buyers or sellers who don't have agents (protecting their own trade, as many professionals do), the difficulty in getting hands-on forms that are required by states to complete sales, and the general misconception by the public that the process can often result in legal trouble without the intervention of a professional. Those of you in the mortgage brokering business know that one tactic frequently used by your industry is to convince consumers that they may not qualify for loans elsewhere or that you have access to more banks and therefore can provide a better service. While there may be some legitimacy to these claims for certain groups of consumers, the vast majority of educated consumers can find a better deal elsewhere. They can turn to online systems to provide the same access to banks, but without the extra fees that you are charging. To compete in this new model, you must change your business plan and give the new breed of consumer more credit—and not in the literal sense.

As real estate professionals are aware, much of their advantage to the consumer comes from their knowledge of market segments or areas. They are not given incentives to save their clients money; contrarily they are given incentives to make the most money for their agency. This is business and making money is important, but it's jeopardized in the new model. As we'll see later, this doesn't necessarily translate to a good equation for the seller of a home, and with the help of the Internet, buyers and sellers are realizing this. Now it's your job to learn how to compete with a more educated seller, and my job is to help you do that.

Real estate agents aren't the only ones who are suffering from an image problem. The same is happening with individuals pursuing a mortgage when they look online and realize their broker wasn't getting them such a hot deal after all. Consumers are finding $450 appraisal fees on their closing statements yet finding out the appraisal really only cost $150. They look at Web sites and compare their closing statements, and see that half the fees they paid were just to generate revenue for various parties and weren't fair to the consumer. Real estate professionals must begin adding value in a Web-enabled marketplace, and this means changing the way you think of your business and how you generate income.

AN AGENT'S WEB SITE

Today, an agent is often forced to have a Web site—either personalized pages on the site of the company you work for or an entirely separate site altogether, just to offer information about yourself, your background, the markets you are most familiar with, and possibly an MLS search capability for the areas you are licensed in. Internet users commonly ask via Web forms or e-mail what commission rates are without even inquiring about the experience of the professional in the area that they want to buy or sell in. This tells you right away what the consumer is concerned with: the bottom line.

Agents tell this story best, noting when asked that sometimes the only question consumers ask is what their commission rate is. Many sellers admit to choosing an agent solely on this criterion alone. Several things have happened that indicate to sellers that the process isn't as difficult as they once thought, and therefore price is what matters and old marketing methods don't work. Technology, the tools available online, and the ability to sell one's own home has grown the for-sale-by-owner market, but has forced agents to decrease commissions or add value some other way just to get listings. A number of new low-commission brokerages online are now also beginning to increase their market share; technology coming out in the next couple of years will only add to their value and diminish that of the traditional real estate professional.

This is yet another indicator that the real estate professionals may, in fact, become a commodity in the future. We see this same trend with mortgage rates; numerous sites devoted to informing the consumer of who has the cheapest loan in their state, and then proceeding to forward them to that lender to process an on-line application, e-mail electronic documents, and provide electronic approvals. Younger people, quite comfortable with the security and reliability of technology and demanding ease in their transactions, are likely to choose this route when buying or selling a home or investment property. Major corporations are betting their future on that, as we'll see and explore.

One model that is used often online today is the lead-generation model. In the lead-generation model, the referring company gets a small referral fee, and the mortgage company or real estate professional gets business as a result. The leads are already "warm," helping weed out those who are truly interested from those who are not, and even screening candidates based on qualifying criteria such as credit score and if they have another home to sell before they can buy. Many leads are already determined as qualifying for a loan or not, indicating both seriousness and ability to follow through. Often information is sent to the lender with qualification documentation so the mortgage company doesn't need to waste its time with a lead that can't be approved for a loan. The entire mortgage is secured without the involvement of real estate professionals to assist and reduce the perceived complication of the process.

FINDING LOANS ONLINE

We can look at real estate and mortgage trade magazines and talk with professionals to understand where their fears are, where the Internet is exploiting the hold real estate and mortgage professionals had on the market, and what the potential impact is. According to the *Real Estate Journal* in August 2004, 55 percent of new home loan seekers searched for their loans on the Internet, yet only 15 percent of banks actually can complete an entire transaction online. This is changing fast—and yet many of you may not have even been aware that 15 percent already can! The companies who are creating Web-based systems are not making you aware of it because they don't want you to compete with it. New standards have created a subset of banks that are going to be capable of supporting the next phase of Web sites that will automate the entire process. While this says a lot about the banking industry and its need to update its systems quickly, no doubt the major banks and lending organizations will adapt to this need as fast as they possibly can. They have no choice, or they will be forced out of the market. So we will assume this trend will continue and the availability of companies completing transactions online will continue growing; this is hardly an assumption anyway, given the market data.

In today's world, individuals expect an immediate response, fast transactions, and no time lost in the process. Chief information officers (CIOs), as noted at conferences and in blogs, have voiced great concern over how to meet the heavy demand consumers place on organizations, particularly with the "immediate gratification," Internet-savvy generation rapidly entering the marketplace.

As this occurs, the relationships that agents have with banks and the potential revenue for both parties diminishes. A new clique is forming that includes those companies that will support the new standards. If you intend to continue competing, you want to be in this clique.

Consumers often don't realize that many agents have partnerships and established relationships: real estate agents with lenders, appraisers with agents, etc. These same types of relationships exist between appraisers and banks, home inspectors and lenders or brokers, appraisers and real estate agents, etc. Real estate professionals recommend other professionals to get transactions through quickly. Sometimes this helps to push through a transaction or even qualify an individual who may otherwise have had a difficult time. This happens in almost all businesses, and real estate isn't immune. Be aware, though, that clients are now questioning whether these partnerships are in their best interest and if they are paying more because of them. Through the Internet, information and negative publicity can be disseminated at an extremely rapid pace, whether it is warranted or not. This helps people understand the processes, but it also puts more pressure on you to be up-front with your clients and remove some of the levels of secrecy involved in the industry.

SEARCHING FOR HOMES

Because many potential buyers depend heavily if not exclusively on the Internet to find homes, anyone selling with or without an agent must advertise his or her home on the Web. Real estate agencies, in an attempt to get listings, proudly talk about all their online services: virtual tours, multiple photos, and fast access to the multiple listing service (MLS). But here is the clincher many people are only now finding out: Doing all these things is easy whether you are selling with an agent or not! Finding a home loan is easy with or without a broker! Many for-sale-by-owner sites offer MLS services so other agents know a home is for sale, and smart agents representing buyers also look at these listings because sellers are advised to note buyer commission rates in their listings. Sellers are becoming more aware that to attract buyers with agents, they must offer commissions, even though most for-sale-by-owner clients don't like doing so. The seller selling a home by owner notes if he or she is willing to work with a buyer's agent and pay the typical 2 percent to 3 percent commission that the buyer's agent usually enjoys. Even though it's still a commission, it is lower than the 5 percent to 6 percent it would cost to use an agent, which could mean thousands of dollars in savings. Many agents won't show their buyers homes with low commission rates; the trouble is they may not have a choice. When your client, the buyer, is bringing you the list of homes he or she saw on the Internet that he or she intends to look at, it is going to be tough to ignore the house or persuade the client to look elsewhere without even seeing the home. You may find reasons to not recommend the house, but ignoring it altogether will be downright next to impossible and suggesting it is not a good home for personal reasons is not ethical. Those who sell by owner are not happy that they have to pay commissions to buyers' agents and are often angered by the limited work the buyers' agents must do. Some sellers may ask the agents to handle the paperwork to try to earn their commissions, while others may flat out refuse to work with agents altogether and work only with individuals who are interested in buying truly by and for owner.

This practice is raising the eyebrow of government agencies and consumer advocates who take issue with this fact. The government is investigating several aspects of the real estate profession, which is discussed in the technology chapter. With the availability of direct buyer-seller tools available online, this need not be the case in the future.

In one personal experiment, I used a popular for-sale-by-owner Web site without listing my home in the MLS. I received just as many inquiries on my home using this method along with a yard sign than by paying the added $300 to $500 to have my home listed in the MLS, which then shows up on the software agents commonly use to search for new listings. Interestingly enough, some (not most) agents still say that "only they" can list homes in the MLS, which is simply not true. Be aware that your consumers are becoming more savvy and aware of the facts regarding what they can and cannot do, and to compete with the tools that will soon be provided to them, you must think differently about your business. As consumers become more aware of the technology and more technologically savvy, and decide they want to keep more of their appreciation in their own bank accounts, you must change your business model and find a way to add value in a market where consumers are questioning what the value is.

COMPANIES THAT CREATED MARKET REVOLUTIONS

In the 1990s, companies such as eTrade revolutionized the way that individuals and experienced investors traded stocks. During this time, we saw other industries from travel to toys also change because of the rapid expansion and integration of technology. We saw buyers and sellers interacting directly under "perfect market" conditions using tools such as eBay, and we saw eToys take a stronghold over the Toys "R" Us market share. We saw travel agents lose their jobs and change industries entirely, and call centers in India pop up for pennies on the dollar to handle routine travel booking transactions through Web sites offering value-added service, like direct hotel communication and hotel research, 24/7 support (try getting that from a travel agent), and a generally reduced cost. Even high-end retail, where "service is king," is being quickly replaced by online e-tailers offering great service at a lower price with often no sales tax and no shipping fee—even free return shipping. Smart retailers are realizing this and providing their own high-end products online; others are waning, consolidating, and buying one another in hopes of surviving.

We are watching as Voice over Internet Protocol (VoIP) companies such as Skype and Vonage take over traditional telecommunications methods and replace them with consumer-friendly, inexpensive alternatives, and get purchased by powerhouses like eBay as a new competitive advantage for an "old" Web business. We see scores of professionals in just about every industry being replaced with Web sites by those consumers who are truly comfortable with the technology.

Today, the Internet is enabling real estate professionals and their associated transactions. Today, technology is your friend, a way to get new clients and to provide them with great response and efficiency. While that will continue for a short while, new versions of technology will also be your number one competitor and enemy. Some individuals still use their stockbroker instead of an online service, but the numbers are dwindling—and that is reflected in the profits of these traditional companies. Their online outfits, however, are doing exceptionally well. Some people still want the comfort of talking to a real estate professional and working with one on a transaction, but many will dismiss the idea as crazy.

Sometimes agents are still involved as they often represent the buyer (after all there is no fee to the buyer to use an agent, therefore the buyer has no motivation to skip the agent like the seller does), but they are representing sellers far less often. After an initial offer, the buyer's agent isn't too heavily involved, especially in the case of for-sale-by-owner transactions where the seller doesn't need help with paperwork, or just doesn't ask for it.

TECHNOLOGY AND INVESTORS

Technology is having a profound impact on both the residential and investment real estate sectors. Mortgages, the process and facilitation of buying and selling homes, insurance, appraisals, etc., are all becoming more cost competitive because of the availability of information to individuals on the Internet and the ease by which consumers can now find these companies, regardless of which state they are purchasing in. On top of all this, the more suppliers there are with the same demand or demand that is just slightly less than the increase in supply, the lower the price will be—which is your income. In a sense, technology has provided such a substantial amount of information that investors aren't limited to real estate investing in the areas closest to their homes as they once were; they can invest anywhere the market is undervalued—and they can make money. In the section on market making in Chapter 7, the tie between technology and investors is explored in great detail, offering one way that you, the real estate professional, may choose to gear your business to compete with what's about to come.

RESISTANCE TO CHANGE

Unfortunately, real estate professionals have been highly resistant to change. A report by Intel, titled "Connected 2001: The transformation of the real estate industry," noted that real estate agents have been the core of the business since the beginning of the century. However, this is changing fast and the consumer is benefiting from this incredible change. You can benefit from the change also, but you must recognize the effort being made by your competitors and be creative in the way you position your business.

Approximately 1.4 million people were licensed real estate agents in 2001, but the dropout rate is high—as is the turnover rate. The tests and courses required to become an agent are arguably not extensive. The same can be said for mortgage brokering, though many of you in both industries will disagree. This lack of barrier to entry, to quote one of Porter's competitive forces, is going to keep new agents coming into the market. Only when demand for them drops, thus income drops, will this supply and demand eventually come to rest at market equilibrium.

An estimated 1.2 million agents are licensed in the United States today, a drop from 2001. Agents are often hired for their people and sales skills rather than their knowledge of real estate, and they tend to be technophobic, resisting the need to adapt technology to their business. This results in a smaller number of agents or agencies getting a majority of the listings and business (the Wal-Martization of the real estate industry) because they are not avoiding technology but embracing it. In the future, adopting technology won't be enough and this trend toward true integration and Web-based transactions has already begun. It's critical for you to reinvent yourself and your business model.

TECHNOLOGY THAT HAS CREATED CHANGE

Numerous technologies have been responsible for the dramatic shift in many industries. Understanding the role each has played in the transformation of industries can help us predict what is about to happen in the real estate market. In this book, I have reviewed many of them as well as their impact on the real estate industry.

High-Speed Internet Access. Affordable high-speed Internet access even in difficult-to-reach areas via satellite, cable, or DSL has provided many homeowners with the capability of searching the Internet even faster than they are used to in their places of business. In the "old days" (prior to five or six years ago), people had to go to work if they wanted to surf the Web fast. Today, a cable connection can net a five-megabit-per-second connection rate—three times faster than a company with a T1 line!

As a result of the high bandwidth availability in homes and businesses, content-rich presentations can easily be downloaded online that include numerous high-quality (therefore large file-size) photos, virtual tours that are easily done with a video camera at home, and brochures in PDF format that are viewable on any platform. While the digital divide (the growing disparity between the haves and have-nots regarding Internet access), most impacting Hispanics and African Americans, is creating a sector of the market eliminated from the use of the Internet, this gap is becoming smaller and more individuals than ever before have access to the Internet.

Online Searching. Search agents have had a considerable impact on the ability to look for data and provide reliable information on the Internet. Google, Yahoo!, MSN, and AOL Search together make up a majority of the searching market, with Google capturing most of the market share. Now it's easy to find an appraiser, for instance, in Austin, Texas, by simply typing in "appraiser Austin." Phone one and bingo, you have an appraiser with no additional markup, and a true unbiased third party who doesn't care if you close the deal or not.

XML. eXtensible Markup Language, commonly known as XML, is a rather technical term many of you may not be aware of. XML determines how data are defined. The industry has agreed on Document Type Definition, known as DTD, as the standard for listing data and property information so they will appear the same on any platform or within any Web browser regardless of where they are hosted. This code has created numerous possibilities for searching any source on the Internet, including nationwide MLSs. Local real estate agents must have broker licenses in the area (or state) that they want to subscribe to an MLS in and then pay an MLS subscription fee. With nationwide searching, one of the advantages agents had in finding property has been eliminated. Even Joe Schmoe homeowner who is selling his house in Riverside, California, can easily list it on the MLS without an agent, suddenly exposing himself to everyone with access, in particular REALTOR.com, which is critical in the online market. Eventually, XML and other languages will lead to true paperless transactions, as they have in many businesses today.

Widely Available Information. Demographic information is imperative for investors wanting low-crime and reasonably high-income areas and primary homeowners looking for good schools. Better yet, it is readily available now thanks to published information, government sites, and census data. Most counties have published information on their employment statistics and other demographic data. Probably most useful, assessor offices publish tax information and data about parcels regularly; even small towns without much infrastructure have incredible information available on liens, taxes, and about any data you could want on a piece of property. This makes it easier to purchase the often-coveted foreclosures or bank repossessions that can make investors the most money. This information is available at a small cost online, and it's creating a greater demand for these homes and less demand for the real estate professional who specializes in foreclosures or bankruptcies.

Paperless Office. Paperless transactions have already had a huge impact on real estate; that will only increase and eventually revolutionize the industry. How many documents did your client sign during your last real estate transaction? Imagine the industry, even one agent, who may have 15 deals going at one time and the paper trails required, not to mention the time-consuming tasks and difficulty in tracking and exchanging data. There are incredible costs in faxing (long distance, paper, ink, etc.) and sending documents overnight. You've seen transactions take place online, such as the ability to open bank accounts and even electronically sign critical documents. This same technology, although enhanced, will revolutionize the real estate industry. This will reduce costs, decrease errors, and make things work a whole lot faster for everyone involved. Thus, digital signatures will need to become more reliable and more legally binding, which is happening now. In addition, Web-based wire transfer companies are popping up, making escrow deposits easier.

File Formats. A few years ago, PDFs were a secure method of transmitting information. Because a person could not easily modify a PDF, it was relatively secure. Today, PDFs are easily modifiable with inexpensive software. However, Universal Forms Description Language, or UFDL, is becoming a new standard to create tamperproof documents that preserve data and formatting. We still need to develop ways to digitally sign these and electronically submit them, but numerous companies are working on this now, and it's one of the last pieces of the complete online transaction solution.

Online Mapping and Geographical Information Systems (GIS). Another critical technology has been the capability of mapping online and viewing actual pictures of locations using tools such as Google Earth and A9. In the next chapter we'll talk about this in more detail, but numerous technologies are available today that will enable consumers to view property from satellite images and overlay a variety of physical structures onto the area they are about to buy into. The consumer can add items such as gas stations, airports, freeways, military bases, etc., to these images to get a virtual, remote picture of what the area is like. As an agent, you need to be aware of these tools, even use them yourself. This is especially helpful to those moving out of their area and to investors looking to purchase property, which often needs to be handled in an expedited time frame while saving money on travel costs. The ability to overlay demographic data such as schools, crime, community information, economic statistics, and addresses on top of the map makes it even more useful. New systems from Zillow.com allow individuals to see a map of an area with comps and expected sales prices on top of it all! Overlaying GIS data on top of demographics has long been used in public health; now it's making its way to real estate. It is a natural progression, but it is happening a little faster than most imagined it would.

Online Transactions. The ability to apply for and retain a mortgage online while being able to compare rates of multiple lenders by submitting one application is a tremendous asset to the homebuyer and investor. In addition, this allows individuals to create their own relationships with lenders, bypassing the one their agent has with a banker or broker and creating long-term partnerships based on trust and expediency. As systems become more secure, online payments will become less of a hassle and less worrisome for those still concerned. While most online transactions are protected (and consumers have been warned against using a company that doesn't offer some level of protection or insurance), some individuals are still worried about conducting banking online. The need to worry over this is becoming less of an issue. By far, more identity theft still occurs by rummaging through trash cans for unshredded documents or sales clerks copying credit card numbers than anything seen online.

Process-driven Web Systems. The entire process of purchasing a home can be handled online today—from finding the home, reviewing the home's features, doing appraisals and reports, performing title searches, locating escrow companies, and even finding a low-cost agent for representation. Today, it's a bit scattered; one company for one thing and a different one for something else. Soon this won't be the case and a single entity will handle the entire transaction.

Wiring funds into escrow accounts is also simple and painless with tools available on the Web. As this becomes more commonplace, additional parties support the tools, and data are regularly exchanged, technology will revolutionize the real estate industry in ways unimaginable by most professionals today. The advent of business-driven tools that mimic the way a transaction is handled but do it in an online fashion revolutionized many businesses through the use of Enterprise Resource Planning (ERP) tools or Customer Relationship Management (CRM) applications. These technologies, when implemented properly, are business driven, that is, they mimic the business model that they are designed to make more efficient. This is being applied now to Web transactions, and this trend is getting stronger.

Processing Complicated Transactions. As technology has advanced and information technology professionals have been increasingly motivated to understand business processes (among the highest paid IT professionals are those who are business consultants and frequently have MBAs), the complicated process of completing a real estate transaction can be successfully completed online. Some of the final barriers to this model were the ability to securely sign documents and notarize and electronically sign and file paperwork, all of which have been worked out and will be released soon. Companies are agreeing on standards being set that secure the ability to complete most transactions electronically.

CULTURE CHANGES

Generation Gap. The elimination of fear and the comfort with online transactions is helping to drive the push toward great changes in the way real estate transactions are handled. In the future, much as younger generations poke fun at older people who still see a teller to deposit money into their accounts, the cohorts younger than them will be appalled at the way they handle transactions in person, slowly and inefficiently. This is especially true for investors who don't have as much emotionally invested in a home purchase as, for example, a first-time homebuyer or homeseller or someone looking to build a life somewhere. As generations grow up learning to use the mouse before going to preschool, this trend will continue—and this should have professionals, especially those who are only beginning their career, worrying. Statistics show that the generation you were born into dramatically impacts how "safe" you feel the Internet is to conduct business on. As younger generations have a greater stronghold on the markets, so will their interest and demand in making things easy and efficient so they can focus their energy and time on something else.

Comfort Factor. More individuals are comfortable with technology today than ever before. Financial companies are backing consumers if they get taken advantage of online. Consumers are aware of the relatively positive statistics associated with Web-based security. Consumers are taking more responsibility than ever in the drive toward a secure online environment because it's easier and more efficient for them. This comfort level is creating an environment in which consumers take no issue with providing sensitive data to a trusted site through their keyboard and they know what to look for to ensure their safety.

Real Estate as an Investment. More and more real estate transactions today involve buying and selling of homes for investment purposes—a full quarter, in fact. Individuals or institutional investors are mainly looking for greater returns and a more stable environment than the stock market has been able to accommodate in recent years. Historically low interest rates and the ability to secure a negative amortization loan with 5 percent to 10 percent down make real estate an ideal investment choice. Many business shows have featured professionals who note that real estate is "the way" individuals feel they are getting something tangible for their money; coupled with low interest rates, many are turning to homes to grow their nest eggs; some individuals are more drastically even doing this in place of their traditional retirement savings. Many are turning to real estate for these highly leveraged investments, and this change is fueling the fire for Web-based transactions.

2

BACKGROUND OF
THE PROCESS

Real estate transactions are extraordinarily involved and complicated. To present a common transaction, let's take a bird's-eye view of the processes involved.

Sellers and buyers go through different processes yet with similar individuals involved. A seller wants to sell a home and begins to evaluate the market. First, he or she must decide to sell the home and determine if he or she will sell by owner or with an agent. For the sake of discussion, we will assume an agent is involved. The seller, going through a variety of channels to find an agent (including searching the Internet, asking friends for referrals, or looking at those magnet to-do lists on the refrigerator), will phone a variety of agents. The seller may be looking for a number of criteria; not far from the top of the list, of course, is price. After comparing numerous agents, the seller settles on one.

Now the agent must come into the home, sign a contract with the seller including an exclusivity agreement, and take pictures of the home. The agent must schedule a virtual tour photographer to take pictures, and the agent may ask that the homeowner make various changes to the home to give it greater appeal. The agent then lists the home in the MLS with pictures, after looking at both the home and comparative analyses to set a price that is agreeable to the seller.

Once this is accomplished, the agent shows the home, holds open houses, and the seller is involved in whatever his or her next transaction will be, whether it is moving to another home or just getting out of the market altogether.

On the other side, a buyer is searching for a home using different methods, including searching the MLS and for-sale-by-owner sites. He or she may also want a buyer's agent, which is representation for his or her end of the transaction. This service is free to buyers, so it's more common for buyers to want agents because they don't have to pay fees, with few exceptions. The buyer's agent is paid out of the commission that the seller pays his or her agent. For instance, if the seller's agent is charging 6 percent, the seller's agent will note the commission rate in the MLS listing at 2.5 percent or 3 percent; the greater the number, the greater the incentive for buyers' agents to bring by their potential buyers. This is part of the vicious cycle that will hold you back as you begin to expand your business!

The buyer finds a home on an online site and asks his or her agent to set up a showing. The buyer views the home and likes it. The buyer's agent then makes a formal offer to the seller, good for a short period of time with conditions. Standard conditions may include an inspection period, subject to appraisal and, of course, funding for the buyer. The buyer is working with lenders and is preapproved for a loan in the amount he or she is looking to spend.

The seller's agent shows all offers to the seller, whether the agent wants the seller to accept them or not. Based on comps and other factors, sellers' agents often advise the sellers on what to counteroffer, to accept the offer, or to outright reject it. A negotiation process begins between the buyer and the seller through their agents. If one party is not represented by an agent, then the party that is represented must work directly with the individuals.

After an acceptable offer is reached, the paperwork goes to title and escrow. These organizations go through a vast array of processes to begin calculating funds required, working with lenders, insurance companies, appraisers, etc. This portion of the real estate transaction is quite involved, and the escrow companies are often left doing a tremendous amount of the work. Lenders must submit final closing statements so that buyers can wire funds, statements are issued to the buyer and to the seller disclosing who is "getting what" and totaling the transaction, and then the parties move to completion. Banks set up loan document signing either personally or through a bank notary; some seasoned individuals may choose to read their own paperwork and sign documents through their own notary.

Once this is completed, some states require a right of rescission, which is the ability to cancel a deal for particular reasons within a given period of time. Once the deal has been funded and the bank sends money to escrow (as well as the buyer, if needed), escrow then records the deed, sends the proceeds to the seller if there are any, and sends back to the buyer any additional funds that were used as padding.

As you all know, this is an oversimplification of the process. The transaction changes hands many times, with many individuals looking at the paperwork. Still we manage to complete millions of transactions per year, and technology today helps us do that.

In 2005, the National Bureau of Economic Research introduced a working paper by Steven D. Levitt and Chad Syverson called, "Market Distortions When Agents Are Better Informed: The Value of Information in Real Estate." Among other fascinating things we can extrapolate, much as Levitt did in his book *Freakonomics,* is that fear drives individuals who sell homes to use real estate agents rather than simply selling homes themselves. Many sellers believe that the process is "too complicated" or "I won't price my house right and it will either stay on the market too long or I'll settle for too little," believing that real estate agents have the perfect information to market and sell their home for the perfect price.

Levitt clearly explains why this is not the case in his book on the practical side of economics, so rather than focusing on this fact, this chapter will educate real estate professionals on the roles and tactics used by others in their profession to maintain their business. This chapter also focuses on the role that information privacy has had in maintaining the real estate market as we know it, and how technology is challenging those walls at every turn.

As with most professions, the more data you can keep to yourself, the better perceived value you offer your clients. Real estate professionals have a self-protective need to share only limited information and that is based on the way that the business used to operate. As the Internet breaks down these barriers, the protection that you have in the marketplace will fade. That is why this book is so important; you need to begin thinking now how you will adapt to the changes occurring in the industry. The sooner you prepare for this and think about what you want your business to look like as the shift occurs, the better off you will be in the long run.

The only valid way for a real estate professional to truly understand what the consumer sees is to know what tools he or she is using and what he or she is thinking. In the following sections, you will learn a bit about what your counterparts in the real estate profession do, and how their jobs are at risk because of technology and a changing marketplace. We must take some time to explore many of the tactics used by various professionals to understand where their previous competitive advantages will no longer hold up in a Web-based marketplace. By understanding one another's profession a bit more clearly, it may enable you to rethink how you partner and who you partner with.

REAL ESTATE AGENTS—THE PROTECTIVE VEIL

Real estate agents have been exceptional gatekeepers of information. In the old days, you carried around books containing infrequently updated listings, which was all the information available to your clients. Today, you use the Internet and e-mails are sent to you automatically when particular houses or homes in specific areas hit the market. What an amazing capability you have at your fingertips! Technology has a tendency to level the playing field, however, and this is quite true for real estate agents. Keep in mind that one of the ways agents have stayed in business is that in general, you've been unwilling to work with sellers who aren't using agents also. Sometimes for-sale-by-owner clients are alienated because they didn't understand they had to offer commissions. Thankfully that is changing and they are better to work with than ever before.

As with most sales individuals in just about any industry, people will act in a way that is in their best interest. If you are a follower of Adam Smith's theories or have taken any sales classes, you already know this. You stand little to gain by getting more for a client's house (assuming you are the seller's agent) by the time you split profits with the buyer's agent and then share a portion with the agency you work for. The idea of having to lower commissions even more seems completely unreasonable, but you have to compete with online organizations that are offering low-rate or flat-fee listings. Just recently, when I was listing a home, a real estate agent told me something that went like this: "With the market like it is and all the competition out there, it would not be possible for me to charge my full commission rate anymore. However, since I need to attract buyers' agents with at least 2.5 percent commission, I still need to charge at least 4.5 percent; 4 percent if I can represent the seller and the buyer."

It's very important for those of you who are not agents to understand how this works, so here's an example. Say a home is listed on the market for $550,000 and the agent is charging the consumer a flat 6 percent commission, or $33,000. Now, they give

50 percent of that, or 3 percent, to the buyer's agent. The $33,000 in commission is split with the buyer's agent, leaving $16,500 for each agent (assuming a 50-50 split, which is often the case). Now the real estate agent has to pay his or her agency, often another 50 percent. The agent ends up with $8,250.

Say a seller gets an offer for $525,000 on the home, a full $25,000 less than the previous asking price. Let's also assume this is lower than the comparable worth, using numbers to show what other homes in your neighborhood have sold for. Yet an agent may still be inclined to push his or her seller to sell the property for this lower price. The reason for this is that the total commission only drops to $31,500. That is split 50-50 with the other agent, leaving $15,750. Then again, another 50 percent split with the agency. The total to the agent is $7,875, only a $375 difference.

Many people even in the real estate industry don't realize this, but this is the way it works. The listing agent (seller's agent) notes how much commission he or she is willing to pay to the buyer's agent in the MLS listing, and the buyer's agent can decide if it's worth pursuing or not. If the commission is under 2 percent, many consider it insulting or a waste of time and won't even look at the property, especially when a seller down the street has a home offering a higher commission rate.

If the seller's agent was able to convince a seller to pay a full 6 percent commission, often 3 percent is offered to attract more potential buyers' agents, therefore more potential buyers. The seller's agent is trying to get a higher commission to attract more potential buyers, not because it makes a major impact on his or her bottom line. The buyers' agents will have more incentive to show potential buyers (their clients) homes that have higher commission rates for them rather than those that fit the clients' requirements best. This is, of course, a fine line; showing a totally inappropriate house isn't good either, even if the commissions are high.

Agents, in an understandable effort to protect their own industry, created a system that doesn't always act in the best interest of their clients. This is important to note because this type of information, previously held in somewhat of a secretive fashion, is now readily available on the Internet. Your clients feel they have a right to be aware of it, and those of you who are real estate agents need to modify your business practice to accommodate a more educated market. This is possible through a variety of means, including new partnerships, focusing on a new market segment, or even dealing with only one particular demographic.

Real estate agents and brokers need to be aware that certain consumer-advocacy groups believe that some of the methods used by agents border on dishonesty and unfair business practices. There are some legitimate business reasons for these methods, but they are becoming questioned because the Internet is making the real estate world more transparent. Why not begin rethinking your business now so that you can increase your bottom line and decrease the scrutiny?

To use a legal phrase referring to corporations, the Internet will pierce the veil of protection of real estate professionals who are competing on the basis of information. One issue with this, however, puts everything into perspective: The information that agents used to once hold secret and therefore was truly invaluable in a transaction isn't so secret anymore. Before the Web days (dare I say prior to just three years ago when the Internet reached a far more advanced stage), "comps" as they are called were available only to agents, appraisers, or lenders. These comps show only what other comparable houses in the area have sold for and provide agents with an idea of what to list a seller's home at. These data are generally used in appraisals, which also indicate what banks are willing to loan on homes. Any average consumer can now readily obtain this information. In future chapters, I will discuss some of the sites that consumers will use to buy and sell their homes. You need to be aware of these sites because they are your first phase of competition. As agents, you need to understand tools that the average consumer uses, know what they do, and what gaps still exist, and then remarket yourselves to fit these gaps using new techniques that will work in a new marketplace.

Remember that for decades, only agents had information on what was selling and what wasn't, and buyers went to agents exclusively to find properties listed on the MLS that they did not have access to. Searching was difficult, and knowing anything about the areas that as a consumer we wanted to be in (or didn't want to be in) was even more time-consuming and frightening, especially when moving to a new town or purchasing a primary residence (as opposed to investors who look for undervalued markets that aren't frequently in the best of areas). Many sites and tools now are available to anyone who wishes to use them to help them price their homes according to market value and their own upgrades, download the necessary forms, find crime statistics and demographics on an area, find an escrow company, and even locate a real estate attorney if the sellers and buyers are more comfortable doing so.

All these steps are functions that real estate professionals used to serve. To compete with this, you need to repackage your services and offer *something new* to the client who can do the legwork with ease on his or her own. This includes mortgage lenders (especially brokers who are already frequently using practices questionable by consumer-interest groups) and others who are involved in the transaction.

REAL ESTATE AGENTS' INCENTIVES

We've already seen how the agents' incentives to sell homes for market value or above are not exactly ready to compete in an Internet-based market. The best salespeople, and I've watched them firsthand, will easily convince a homeowner to take less for his or her home because it's "in their best interest" and "if we don't take this offer we may not have another." But this is not a fact in most markets where demand far exceeds supply. If you simply manage the buying and selling of properties, you will find yourself replaced with online home seekers who feel more than confident with a few tools available to them (many for free) to complete the transaction themselves. Sellers are often unaware of this and don't put your motives into perspective, which is detrimental to the financial state of the seller. But they are beginning to, and technology that used to be of great benefit will now also be a competitive threat. The Internet is beginning to change this, and now you will need to find new ways to compete in a market where sellers are aware of what is in *their* best interest.

Even though all this information is becoming available to consumers over the Internet, is it worth it to the consumer to forgo services provided by professionals? As the Internet grows and it becomes easier to complete these transactions online, consumers may choose the convenience over the personal attention. At this point, the Internet has simply advanced the education level of consumer sellers and buyers. To not realize this or pretend this is not happening will not be beneficial for any involved professionals, because it's better to know what you're dealing with and learn how to compete than to ignore it and go out of business one day.

One of the few remaining annoyances for buyers and sellers in real estate transactions is the time involved in reading and interpreting paperwork. It may be less work for consumers to sell through an agent, but the cost benefit has to be there for the consumer. Paperwork that is often most troubling for consumers includes the initial documents that the seller signs to list a home with an agent, the itemized list of potential issues with the home, the final closing statements, and the lender's paperwork. Sometimes the paperwork is confusing, particularly if the consumer doesn't know what to look for or is an average homeowner who buys and sells every few years. Still, many individuals may value their time over the savings of doing things on their own, so this may be a competitive advantage over the Internet in some marketplaces and with some demographics.

To help solidify my thoughts in this book, I conducted some firsthand research of real estate professionals that is discussed more thoroughly later. It was clear, however, that those of you who are real estate agents are marketing yourselves as doing more than just paperwork. If you are one of these agents, you will need to document exactly what the added value is. Unless the buyer lives in a difficult-to-sell area (and there aren't many of those around these days) or interest rates reach 1980s levels, the value added may not be enough for some sellers. By analyzing numerous transactions and for-sale-by-owner home sales, it is reasonable to conclude these agents and other professionals are not realizing the potential change that the Internet will introduce. Online competitors are knocking down the walls that agents have spent many decades building.

The newest ad campaigns I expect agents and their respective companies to put out in the foreseeable future will focus on how the agents and their companies take the guesswork out of the process, and find buyers who are suitable. The truth is, buyers can find homes without agents, and quite easily. In fact, many (nearly most) of the buyers bring homes they found themselves to their agents! Sellers can list their homes on the MLS, make modifications, upload pictures, create virtual tours, and do just about anything else the agents often say that only they can do. Your new marketing campaigns must have the seller's interest at heart and must assume an educated consumer and not a passive one. Many of you do add value to the traditional role, but most of you will have to step up to the Internet age of an educated or at least more informed consumer to make this value perceived the way you want it to be by the buyers and sellers.

Remember, not all that long ago, buyers wanting to find homes needed an agent to see what was available. Agents often show properties that are for sale by their own clients (that gives them the full commission rather than splitting it with the buyers agent). If the buyer isn't biting or nothing fits well, the agent goes to work finding a home where he or she doesn't get the full commission, but where commission rates are at least on the high end (close to 3 percent). To attract these buyers' agents, this also means the seller's agent has to convince the seller to pay as high a commission as possible, because if he or she doesn't do this, the agent will have a harder time attracting other agents to the home. Agents will point out the best features of the home and strategize with the seller's agent to find out what the homeseller may drop the price to. As an agent, you lose little money by getting the seller to drop the price, and you create a trust relationship with the buyer should he or she sell a home in the future or perhaps even an immediate sale with the home he or she is moving out of. This is fine, but keep in mind that consumers are running their own comps, they know what their neighbor sold for even if they've never spoken a verbal word to him or her, and they expect to see results.

Right now, some may argue that it's in the seller's best interest to *not be up front* with you about what his or her bottom-line price is because it quite possibly may be shared with the buyer's agent, although most agents will consider this unethical. If you want your clients to be honest with you, you will need to create an environment in which they have reason and reward for being honest. Sellers fear that if you know their bottom lines, you will show them offers only slightly above or at the bottom lines rather than working harder to get more money for their homes. This happens all the time and sellers regularly confide this, and one of the barriers agents have used to protect their system is their well-kept information. No longer!

THE INTERNET MARKETPLACE

In the new Internet marketplace, some consumers and their advocacy groups are asking why so many people need to get a piece of the real estate pie. Recently, a homeseller asked me why there were so many fees on the final closing statement. I joked that the banks used Exxon as their appraisers. The seller continued, "Pay $450 for an appraisal?" Any consumer who has thoroughly read closing statements knows that many hands touch the transaction, and each one gets paid.

The new Internet marketplace doesn't just make individuals aware of this, it actually asks them not to pay it. It asks them to use flat-fee or low-cost agents to complete transactions, and then "at least money will be saved somewhere." The fees aren't going away, but as with any industry almost anytime information technology is involved, costs of doing business go down. If an online selling agent uses an e-escrow company that charges half of what you charge, that is just one more incentive for the seller to use online services to sell his or her home.

Often you may recommend an escrow company, one that may be affiliated with your real estate organization. Fees are sometimes given to either you or the agency you work for. This holds true for appraisers, notaries, banks, home inspection companies, you name it—anyone involved in the transaction has a high probability of being chosen because it's in the best interest of you, the real estate professional. Now you will need to modify your practices to show your clients how you are actually saving them money and providing better service and value.

Banks have relationships with many of these same organizations. The loser in this "deal" is the buyer and the seller, who are stuck paying whatever fee the companies charge while feeling intense pressure to use those who are "automatically chosen for them." So in the new marketplace, a key to success is officially, truly, and deeply changing the way you offer your services and the value you provide. Buyers and sellers are starting to realize that many of the fees and service charges they pay are actually negotiable, and this will hurt your bottom line if you're not careful. Remember that in an Internet marketplace, many of the services you are offering are going to become a commodity and price is going to be more of an issue than ever before. The buyer and seller just want to save money. As home prices go up, a percentage of the home sale as commission is also going up, and fewer people are willing to pay that.

MORTGAGE BROKERS

Real estate professionals have long known the value of mortgage brokers. If you are not a mortgage broker, this section will help you understand what brokers do and how they make money. If you are a broker, this section should help you begin to think about how others perceive your business in the Internet era, and how you may help change these perceptions.

No doubt, you assist in certain transactions and really help individuals who need service for various reasons. Unfortunately, by nature, the way you do business is causing some people to call foul, and this is especially true on the Internet where thoughts and opinions are readily shared and where anyone is an instant expert.

Mortgage Professor on Yahoo! Finance, written by Jack M. Guttentag, addresses a question many people ask—What exactly does a mortgage broker do? In his words, "A mortgage broker is an independent contractor who offers the loan products of multiple lenders who are called 'wholesalers.' A mortgage broker counsels you on the loans available from different wholesalers, takes your application, and usually processes the loan, which involves putting together the complete file of information about your transaction including the credit report, appraisal, verification of your employment and assets, and so on. When the file is complete, but sometimes sooner, the lender 'underwrites' the loan, which means deciding whether or not you are an acceptable risk. And it is the lender who shows up at the closing table with the money, not the mortgage broker."

Many in the real estate profession don't even understand how mortgage brokers make money, and mortgage brokers don't readily share this information with consumers. The Internet, though, is making it clear how this occurs, and, as that trend continues, mortgage brokers will be hurting more for business than before.

The lenders that mortgage brokers work with are wholesale lenders and therefore offer wholesale prices to the broker. It's up to the broker to add a markup to create a retail price that is then offered to the consumer. For instance, as Guttentag notes, the wholesale price on a particular program might be 7 percent (interest rate) and zero points (fee paid up front as a percentage of the loan cost to buy down the interest rate, eliminate prepayment penalties, or a variety of other things). The broker, for instance, can then add a markup of one point, resulting in an offer to the consumer of 7 percent and one point. If the broker adds a two-point markup, the resulting offer is 7 percent plus two points. Interest rates, points, and fees are all up fair game by the broker. While there is more room to negotiate with brokers than with direct lenders, the consumers are almost always paying more, except in certain cases. Often brokers will set a number as high as they believe the consumer will allow them to.

The poorest individuals, or those with the least desirable credit ratings, often feel as though they won't be able to get a loan elsewhere and may take these deals, even if there are lenders that *will* directly help them. Mortgage brokers need to understand that while some clientele, usually those mentioned previously, may continue to use your services, as rates increase and the market naturally adjusts itself, coupled with the amazing amount of information available on the Internet, your place in the market will be uncertain. More and more, mortgage brokers have found their buyers threatening to back out at the last minute after all the paperwork has been done when they found the same type of loan cheaper online or directly through a lender.

Many people don't realize that mortgage brokers don't have a pool of money that they lend themselves. Despite this, one major benefit to the consumer of going with a mortgage broker is that the broker is able to shop many lenders, perhaps 30 or more, and sometimes that will truly result in a better price for the consumer. Many people don't have the time, know-how, or patience to comparison shop, and if a consumer doesn't buy and sell homes regularly, he or she may not have established relationships with lenders for the best deals. These types of consumers are a great niche market for the mortgage broker.

In the new Internet marketplace, you make your value abundantly clear to consumers and honestly reveal where you are making money; but most important, you reveal where you are saving the consumer money—in the added fees the lender may charge that the broker does not or perhaps because the wholesale rates plus a commission are even lower than the retail rates, which is the case sometimes. Creating return analyses showing each model (direct to lender and through the broker) may help educate consumers on the differences in what they are paying over, for example, 15 or 30 years. Still, consumers are becoming more aware that the money you are making is the difference between what the lender actually charges and what you can sell the loan for. Many question whether you have the best interest of the vast majority of your clients at the heart of your business. If you don't, rethink it because the Internet will expose it.

Mortgage brokers need to be keenly aware that *many Internet sites are telling consumers how to find ethical brokers,* as well as which practices are considered ethical and which ones aren't. Chapter 6 on what real estate professionals can "do about all of this" will provide ways in which you can be seen in the marketplace as an ethical broker, and therefore have a shot at competing with an Internet-based market. You should also be aware that the Mortgage Professor, a commonly referred to site by investors and buyers, lists a very small group of mortgage brokers he believes to be up-front mortgage brokers. This list is available at *www.mtgprofessor.com/* in the up-front mortgage broker section. If you aren't already familiar with it, you should become so quickly. While it's not necessary for you to buy into his program, many of the practices he explains hold true for any lender or broker.

LENDERS

Lenders are competing in perhaps one of the tightest markets we've seen in a long time. You are competing against brokers who are working with many wholesale lenders, and you are also competing with the Internet—a constant nemesis that is getting worse and not going away. A lot of data appear on the Internet about the lending process, what lenders do (loan money to people who want to buy primary residences, second homes, or investment properties), and how to find a reputable one who won't rip off the consumer. If you haven't already, you should read these sites regardless of what profession you are in. If you are an agent and recommend a particular lender or broker, you need to expect that your clients, for example, will be reading up on the individual you are recommending and even comparing his or her rates with those online. Sites such as bankrate.com offer consumers lots of information about current mortgage rates, as does Yahoo!'s Finance site and many others.

One area that has boomed with low interest rates and high demand for housing are subprime lenders, lenders who qualify borrowers who don't qualify for loans with mainstream lenders. More often now we are seeing these mainstream companies opening additional organizations, perhaps under different names, offering subprime lending.

Prices are a dead giveaway that a lender is subprime, and consumers are becoming more and more aware of this. While individuals with low credit scores may have no choice but to use subprime lending, they are becoming more aware of the drawbacks of doing so, and more online banks are offering these same individuals much better deals. If you are a lender, particularly a subprime one, you must be acutely aware of what is being said about your business and how you will counter it with accurate and useful information that's helpful to your clients.

In this section, we'll talk about the different type of loan officers and the ways that banks make money. This is important because your clients, regardless of your position in real estate, may ask you for information. Loan officers, whether they work for brokers or lenders, are essentially commissioned salespeople. Lenders are further segmented as either mortgage bankers or portfolio lenders. Mortgage bankers sell the loans that they close in the secondary market because the amount of money needed to hold the loan for the long term is too high for them. They actually fund by borrowing from banks themselves on short-term notes and then repay them. Mortgage banks are dominant in the U.S. markets. Of the ten largest lenders last year, nine were mortgage banks and one was a portfolio lender. Many of the large mortgage banks, such as Chase Manhattan Mortgage and Wells Fargo Mortgage, are actually affiliated with large commercial banks (Guttentag, 2006).

A portfolio lender includes many subsets of lenders: commercial banks, savings banks, savings and loan associations, and credit unions to name a few. They usually offer deposit accounts to the public that provide a stable source of funding to allow them to place permanent loans in their portfolio and not resell the loans on the secondary market. Consumers find this more appealing sometimes because when banks are constantly selling loans, they can be in a position where they are literally making a payment to a different bank every month for many months on end. It's very frustrating, especially to the investor who is juggling multiple lenders and loans. Of the top ten largest lenders, Washington Mutual (known as WAMU in the industry), a savings bank, is the only depository bank on the list.

In general, Internet data tells us that mortgage banks offer better terms on fixed-rate mortgages than portfolio lenders do, while the opposite is true for adjustable-rate mortgages. However, there is a great degree of variability in this "rule of thumb" that we can read about on the Internet.

A popular Internet site already mentioned, Mortgage Professor, discusses many of the pros and cons to shopping online, teaches consumers how to find up-front brokers, tells how to avoid being ripped off by lenders, and is considered a consumer-friendly reputable site. You should visit this site, which is discussed in later chapters, to understand better what type of information your clients are regularly reading and easily obtaining. Lenders have less control over their business because most often they work for a big company and have to sell a product that is offered by their organization with rates set by people much higher in the company than they are. Finding ways to compete online as a lender will be up to your organization and how it handles Web-based business. You will want to find this out, ask questions, and make decisions accordingly about whom you want to work for.

APPRAISERS, TITLE, AND ESCROW

Often overlooked in discussions or books on real estate professionals, appraisers play a major role in any real estate transaction. Some can be found online now, "neutral" third parties not recommended by any agent or bank. Many consumers are now crying conflict of interest at every turn of a real estate transaction.

There is an inherent conflict of interest with agents choosing appraisers. Take for instance the home for sale at $550,000 mentioned earlier. If the appraisal doesn't come in at $550,000, there is a good chance the bank won't approve the loan. One clause in most real estate contracts is a loan contingency and/or an appraisal contingency within a given period of time, meaning that if the home doesn't appraise for the value it's being purchased at, then the buyer can back out of the deal without losing anything.

A buyer's agent doesn't want the buyer to back out of a deal. From my experience, most appraisers, afraid of being flagged as overvaluing homes (after being accused of doing so for years) are actually undervaluing now (contrary to about two years ago when they appeared to be overvaluing in general, though no solid proof of that seems to exist). There is an inherent conflict of interest when the buyer's or seller's agents are choosing the appraisers. Of all the players in the games, banks are probably the least likely to be biased, though they will tend to err on the side of conservatism because they don't want to get taken to the cleaners if the owner files for bankruptcy. Unfortunately, some in the real estate business have colluded with each other and convinced sellers to sell based on a low appraisal, in the process closing a deal quickly but leaving the seller with less than he or she should have and lowering the overall comps in the area.

The Internet has changed this, and buyers and sellers can run a comparative analysis themselves without much difficulty. They have been told by numerous online companies that if the appraisal looks fishy, it probably is. They may double-check your work, or even get their own appraisal first. If their neighbor's house of comparable size and upgrades sold for $20,000 higher than their appraisal came in at, they may refuse the offer or get another appraisal. In this new market, appraisers must act in a truly unbiased and fair way and must not have such direct relationships with agents or banks that they are biasing their values toward any one party. In the new Internet age, this will disrupt your business.

Simply put, real estate professionals will be less valuable as firsthand information is available and the public becomes more aware of many of the tactics various professionals use to increase fees and not necessarily accommodate with increased service.

All real estate professionals, regardless of their place in the business, will need to modify their practices to adapt to the Internet age. Imagine a market with perfect information: What will this do to your business? You must find a niche and a way to add value or risk becoming obsolete, drastically lowering commissions or finding a new market sector to work in (such as investors who are more prone to have to rely on agents to sell homes in areas they do not live in). This is not impossible, but it requires fast, creative thinking.

Title and escrow companies are also in a similar quandary. Individuals will soon be able to obtain all these services online while paying very low fees, and most certainly the tie that these agencies have with banks or agents will be useless to these Internet-based consumers. If you are in this business, you should get your systems up to speed with the new standards and align yourselves with organizations—online companies—that will begin offering online services and complete transaction packages. The work on your part initially might be intense as you get your systems up to speed, but your business will be so streamlined you will quickly see why the costs are lower.

Individuals can get information easily, and soon they will be able to conduct the entire real estate transaction online. If you are a real estate professional and have read through this chapter, you must by now be convinced of the need to change how you do business. Now we will start preparing you to do just that, think outside the box, and get ready for tomorrow's technology.

3

THE INTERNET—TURNING SERVICES INTO COMMODITIES

Many industries have been severely impacted by technology and, specifically, the Internet or, as we commonly refer to it, the World Wide Web (WWW). Often these changes have led to products or services becoming commodities with vendors or partners chosen based on price and not much else.

The Internet poses a risk to the value of services you as real estate professionals offer your clients. As with many industries, services are quickly becoming commodities in a world where the lowest price wins. How many times have your clients asked you what the interest rate is before they ask about your experience? Or they inquire about your commission rate before they ask how long your houses have been on the market compared to the average for your area? The Internet has created a marketplace in which every product and service can be offered cheaper, thanks to the efficiency the technology has provided and being able to sidestep the middleman. This same risk is applicable to real estate professionals in all fields as technology changes the value placed on your service, moving from a face-to-face model to a more efficient and impersonal online model.

This chapter is essential in forming the foundation that, in the future, the real estate industry will follow. Other markets and sectors as well as purchases will be made using new tools to compare prices and offer fast service with information readily available online. By the end, you will be convinced that, in fact, a substantial risk of this happening in real estate is quite possible and the groundwork has already been laid. I am certain you are aware of the low-cost or flat-fee agents in your area advertising heavily on semitrucks on major highways, or the commercials asking the consumer if they are tired of paying high real estate fees. Now it's time to do something about it. Know the value you add, and then sell the heck out of it.

Interestingly enough, not too long ago the Internet in its infancy created a market in which *products* became commodities; online companies appeared everywhere that compared prices (such as Bottomdollar.com and PriceGrabber.com) and helped the consumer choose the cheapest of all the stores, including shipping and tax considerations, for nearly any product imaginable. Many of us cannot imagine shopping for any major purchase without first going to the Internet and looking at the prices online. In the latest round of Web updates, however, we're seeing *services* also hit with this commoditization of industry, and this drastically affects real estate.

Earlier in the book, I mentioned the technology of Voice over Internet Protocol, or VoIP. VoIP, which may not be a household acronym, has eaten away at telecommunication companies' profits for telephone service and long-distance service and is often a *free* option that individuals or businesses can get online. Have you heard of Skype or Vonage? These companies are slowly eroding the markets of local and long-distance service providers. We're seeing this across numerous industries; travel, high-end retail, stock trading—the lists go on and on.

Can you think of what it was like before the Web allowed online travel booking and searching multiple airlines for the best (and cheapest) flights? How many people use Expedia.com or Travelocity.com or the numerous other sites similar to these to find the cheapest, fastest flight from point A to point B? In fact, you probably do it yourself. How do you feel about using a travel agent; does the information the agent has on the best hotels he or she has stayed in warrant paying more money and taking more time to complete a transaction without the ease of making modifications with the touch of a button? Sometimes, but rarely is this the case.

Let's take another example of where free services are filling a market niche. Imagine a single voice mail box provided by some telecom companies that, perhaps, might tack on an additional $5 to your phone bill. Why pay $5? Did you know you can forward your cell phone to free services that will allow you to receive your voice mail in a file by e-mail when you're traveling, without paying international roaming rates to your cell phone provider? Or the telecommunication provider's fee for the single voice mail box? You can even return the call free on the Internet using a microphone and your built-in laptop speaker. What about the possibility of comparing hundreds of vendors simultaneously, including shipping fees, by simply going to one Web site and typing in a part number or product description after doing all your research on opinion and vendor sites, such as Bottomdollar and PriceGrabber as I previously mentioned? These and many more tools are available now for consumers. Their use is growing steadily and spiking in many market sectors.

CHANGING INDUSTRIES

The Internet has changed many industries to being commodity based; those with the lowest price, fastest shipping, and best return policies win—period. Companies such as Zappos.com and Shopbop.com have been extremely successful in markets no one thought possible just a few years back because of their extraordinary customer service; it's actually easier to return to these

companies than it is to most retailers. Some brick-and-mortar retailers figured this out and created online stores that also have
exceptional policies, and many are doing quite well. They capitalized on the fact that a consumer doesn't need to mail in his
or her returns; they can choose to do so or they can take them
to the nearest retail store. Ah, a competitive advantage! You
need to find these in your business. Even eBay has created a
"perfect market" as its creator intended by connecting buyers
and sellers directly without the middleman so that, in theory, the
buyer is paying exactly what that item is worth at that moment
and the seller is receiving funds equal to the value of that product at the moment it is sold. Economists marvel at the research
data available by studying companies such as eBay because they
are creating markets like we've never seen before. Online eBay
stores essentially created a forum for the middlemen to charge a
fixed price or allow auctions on their goods, but even that has
changed the way these middlemen are doing business, often
working out of small offices or their garages to store their inventory and hiring low-wage workers to post pictures online. In fact,
I know many people who ship directly from online retailers who
have hard-to-find products, only using eBay as their online store
to make a markup! This is a creative way to be a middleman, but
it may be temporary. Eventually, something better and cheaper
will come along, and the best of the best will adapt.

How many companies have both brick-and-mortar and online
stores? Few have been successful in doing so, but Barnes & Noble
quickly comes to mind. Barnes & Noble has a successful online
store and a successful brick-and-mortar store; they both thrive in
a competitive market. Very few companies have successfully navigated this transition. It is difficult to do, and your product or service must be suitable to both the click-consumer and the brick-
consumer, and you must cater to both if you want to work in both
markets. Think of the incredible advantage having both a traditional and an online store offers. Among the benefits are tremendous inventory, on-demand shipping, and convenient returns for
customers. Your business, whatever your real estate profession,

also has these advantages—you just need to creatively think to uncover them.

Think of the rapid change in how middlemen are used even with popular retail stores. When you order from an online store, is it shipping from the store or directly from the vendor? Try ordering shoes from Nordstrom.com and see how often the box comes from Nordstrom itself and how often the box comes directly from the warehouse. The online store Nordstrom.com often acts as a simple middleman storefront for the consumer, much like the Barnes & Noble's online store has. Shipping direct to the consumer from the manufacturer or a large warehouse is a fast and common way to handle online transactions.

What about industries where there is no need for a middleman? Nordstrom adds value by allowing the consumer to return to an actual store and avoid shipping fees, providing prewritten labels (some companies offer prepaid labels, too), and providing the same customer service online that its brick-and-mortar stores are known for. It answers e-mail within hours, phones customers when required, and almost always addresses even difficult questions about product location or ordering promptly. In real estate, you must find your own way to add value, much in the way that these successful retailers have. Many consumer groups argue that real estate agents, thus far, have simply looked out for themselves and avoided customer service altogether unless it brings additional commissions. Do you want to continue this perception consumers have while adding competition at the same time? This is surely a death threat to your business.

THE INTERNET CAN HELP, TOO!

The Internet on the outside may look like an overwhelming, even formidable contender for your business. But, interestingly, mortgage lenders are looking to the Internet to help reduce fraud and make transactions more secure. According to the *Los Angeles Times* on December 5, 2005, the FBI reported that mortgage fraud reports have tripled to 21,994 annually, with the dollar value of these crimes quadrupling to $1.01 billion. The reporter's research indicates that the run-up in the housing market coupled with low interest rates has encouraged individuals to do such things as lie on applications about income, use fake appraisals, and employ straw buyers to steal properties from unsuspecting owners. Mortgage companies, unhappy about the government trying to regulate their industry, rarely report mortgage fraud.

Brokers have a reputation for swindling their customers in the online community, yet an unprecedented number of loan applicants are using them. This is in part because of their willingness to do unconventional things, such as increase the interest rate when the client will hold the property short term and receive a large kickback from the bank that is then shared with the consumer. Banks don't like this because it means that the client will likely turn the loan over quickly, and the bank ultimately loses money because it costs a lot of money to initiate a loan. The borrower doesn't keep the loan long enough to make it up with interest payments. A common question on mtgprofessor.com is whether or not it's permissible for borrowers to work with brokers to receive a premium when a loan funds at an overpriced interest rate.

Using the Internet can help control such concerns. For instance, new software will allow lenders to look at the income on the loan application versus the income noted on applications for cars or other smaller items to determine potential fraud. Databases of brokers who bend the rules will also be accessible, thus eliminating them from the pool of potential business partners. Consider this if you are doing things those banks won't like! Software will also allow businesses to obtain additional data on an individual. One method investors use to lower their interest rates is to state that a home is their primary or secondary residence when it's really an investment property. One "red flag" that a property is really for investment purposes is when multiple utility bills are opened in one individual's name or Social Security number. Lenders haven't had these tools at their disposal, but they soon will. These tools require technological integration, which we're creating now. Raising red flags early allows lenders to reduce fraud. Several other technologies will be deployed in the next year to help reduce this problem, as well as make adjustments in interest rates or demand a loan be paid in full if the lender finds that fraud was committed.

IS THE INTERNET A FAD?

Primary research that I've conducted has revealed that some professionals in the real estate business still believe that the Internet is just a fad that will eventually disappear or become less important, reverting back to the olden days when the value of a face was more important. In fact, banks tried this tactic with their consumer-friendly service rather than ATMs. This works for the older generation who is generally more afraid of technology or for those who don't have access or have incredibly slow access, or those who simply have more time on their hands than they know what to do with. How many people can we say, who are purchasing or selling real estate regularly, fit any of these categories?

Studies revealed that, in fact, younger generations didn't *want* the people contact—they want ATMs that do everything for them, plus being highly accurate and fast. Some companies, aware of this exciting change and need, have adapted to the new requirements of today's Internet age. Bank of America has stepped up to that requirement. Rather than trying to convince people that the old way is better, it has put money into research and developed an ATM scheduled to be released in late 2006 or 2007 that will provide more power instantly to the consumer while reducing its costs. It has realized that relatively few transactions require human contact, and the bank will provide this contact when it is required. Simple ATM transactions, just as simple home purchases or sales, do not. While it may seem a stretch to some to compare depositing a payroll check into the ATM to buying or selling a home, it is easily argued these individuals have been listening to too many commercials from real estate agencies trying to convince them otherwise, and apparently the marketing worked for some time. The transparency of the ease with which these transactions really can be done will become more visible, as is always the case when information is made available.

THE TRAVEL INDUSTRY—WILL REAL ESTATE FOLLOW?

Has any traditional service industry been more affected by the Web than the travel industry? Hugo Burge on Cheapflights.com in 2003 noted that Amazon.com (and the Internet) has done amazing things for readers; however, bookstores still exist. To continue quoting the author, Google has reinvented the way we search for information, but libraries still exist and new ones are being built every day. Even though eBay created a new perfect international marketplace and instantly sellers have a global presence and can sell all over the world, the malls are seeing record profits. The mall still adds value as a social gathering place, offering food that is tough to buy through a monitor, and the ability to see and feel something before purchasing it. The mall also offers a service element that some still enjoy. The travel industry, however, has been dramatically changed by technological revolution in much the same way that the real estate sector will be in the future, because it never offered this added value and neither do real estate professionals. This should be a wake-up call to real estate professionals to change the way you practice in this new market or risk facing the same fate that travel agents have been handed.

On searching the Web, you'll find that every single airline has an Internet presence—every single one. Many of the smaller travel agencies have been the ones most impacted by the Internet. Thousands have been forced into bankruptcy or closure because the Internet caught a huge market sector, greater than the travel agents at the time had anticipated. When the Internet was becoming more widely used, travel agents created Web sites that allowed their clients to book trips. Does this sound familiar? Real estate agents are creating links to their local MLS service, making lots of virtual tour movies, putting up online spreadsheets, and searchable databases everywhere. But this is not enough.

What happened with travel? Well, the agents were virtually eliminated; only the strong survived, which included those with corporate partnerships (with extraordinarily decreased fees, sometimes as low as $15 for a company to book an entire trip including trip insurance). Keep in mind that the strong were very few, and almost always did not include small companies. What does this mean for real estate? You guessed it, a lot more than real estate professionals have bargained for or have expected. You have fought so hard to keep outsiders in their place and you've conducted such complicated transactions that yours is one of the last industries to evolve into the Internet age, but it is inevitably happening. Until this book was written, agents had no way to equate their industry to others so they can make the changes necessary to stay in business over the long haul.

Consumers had very little information, all in one place, on how to get help completing transactions online. While this may seem contradictory, it isn't. The revolution on the Internet and the education of the population on real estate transactions is going to happen anyway, so it's up to you—the professionals—to adapt.

Still, a majority of you are following the advice of groups who are supposed to be looking out for your interests, frantically getting better e-mail and Web sites up and running rather than following the model of the individuals who successfully navigated the travel business and creating partnerships, finding new and creative ways to add value, and making themselves something other than a commodity in the process. Strong marketing, innovative approaches to finding niche markets, and quality reputations helped in their survival and these things will also help you.

ONLY THE STRONG SURVIVE

We can find so many parallels in real estate to the travel industry that it's difficult to stay away from the topic for long. One of the advantages travel agents often had is the ability to book an entire package that offered travel discounts, transfer vouchers at the airport, etc. Have you visited online travel booking sites lately that will book an entire trip? Or even American Airlines at *AA.com* for that matter? Most online travel companies (even the airlines themselves) offer packages, thus eliminating one of the competitive advantages agents had over vacationers or business travelers booking trips themselves. In fact, the consumer is often rewarded with additional mileage or club points by booking an entire trip through one airline's Web site! Another advantage agents had was an individual to phone in case a change was needed. The Internet quickly followed with e-mail that allowed you to click to modify a reservation online in seconds.

The same change is happening in real estate. If you are a real estate agent, you may know escrow companies and appraisers, and possess a packet of forms that seem oddly mysterious and frightening to consumers. Online escrow companies (in use on eBay for years to sell big items such as cars and real estate) are popping up in more traditional real estate models. Forms are available on form Web sites for every single state for a mere $40 to $50, or consumers may even find them for free if they're willing to hunt around for an hour or two on Google. Again, does this transformation sound vaguely familiar? Just like the travel agents did, real estate professionals have been ignoring the facts, which will put many out of you flat out of business. You offer a value to your clients, and you need to do what you can to improve and protect your business and your clients. Stop trying to catch up with today's technology and embrace what the future holds. Find new ways to market yourselves and innovative approaches to your business. In this type of Internet-savvy world, creativity is key. Changes will particularly hit the smaller real estate organizations that don't have significant national branding. Look again at

Michael Porter's Five Forces Model, one often recognized by business experts as defining the competitive advantage of a firm. One of these is barriers to entry into the market. The Internet is eliminating this barrier, because the primary one was access to information, and slowly breaking down the others as well.

THE INTERNET'S IMPACT ON PROFITABILITY

According to research, a positive correlation exists between airlines with a strong percentage of their sales coming from the Internet and profitability. There are many reasons for this; however, this fact cannot be ignored. In the future, we will see this trend in real estate as well. Companies are able to directly build relationships with the consumers of their services through the Internet. When was the last time a consumer used you as a real estate agent and started building a relationship with your escrow officer himself or herself, unless you had a difficult transaction to deal with or a buyer or seller who obsessed over the transaction? Probably a long time, if ever. Who does have the relationship? You do, the agent that consumers choose to represent their interests. Why shouldn't buyers and sellers build their own relationships, eliminate the middleman, and work directly with these service providers? They are starting to, and this is yet another battlefront that you must be aware of. This is especially true for real estate investors who will handle more transactions in a year than many primary residence owners conduct in a lifetime.

EXAMINING STATISTICS

Let's look at some statistics regarding the travel market in the United States as of November 2004. Jupiter Research projected travel sales would end the year 2005 at $68 billion. Of this, 27 percent of these dollars would come from online domestic travel sales. That is more than a 20 percent year-over-year increase above the 2003 total. This trend is expected to continue. What would happen if the same numbers suddenly hit the real estate market? That will happen as technology allows us to complete transactions without face-to-face human involvement. Both com-Score Networks and PhoCusWright corroborated the outlook from JupiterResearch. All predict that through 2010, robust growth is expected to continue, reaching a total of $104 billion or 34 percent of all travel purchased will be through online means. JupiterResearch released the following projections through 2010:

Year	U.S. Online Travel Booking Revenue	Percentage of Total U.S. Travel Revenue
2005	$68 billion	27%
2010	$104 billion	34%

Other organizations have been even more optimistic about the online travel market. PhoCusWright's *Online Travel Overview,* released in June, projected the online travel market will grow even faster, noting, "In the United States, this $190 billion industry will see more than half of its total business booked online by 2006." This creates a major shift of jobs from those actually booking travel to other types of jobs, such as technology designing, creating, and supporting the online systems. It seems the place to be is in technology, not in the travel industry. Just as the travel industry professionals must create a niche to survive, so must the real estate professionals. The tug-of-war between suppliers who can offer direct services and third parties who act as middlemen is heating up because of the Internet, and this battle is favoring the consumer. In an economy such as ours, the consumer will always win.

More recent information from the same group has reported even more astounding figures. According to ZDNet Research, JupiterResearch has found that the U.S. online travel market has experienced incredibly strong growth in the past year and this is expected to grow to $104 billion in 2010.

Certain sectors of the market, demographically speaking, are more likely to turn to the Internet for major purchases, such as cars, travel, and homes. In the travel industry, numbers are rising for the 18-to-34 age group more rapidly than for any other. For instance, in travel, 13 percent of those over 50 used primarily travel Web sites as of August 2002; however, this number was 32 percent for those in the coveted 18-to-34 category. Additional information on this topic can be found on CNET News.com, "Online travel bookings on the rise" (Kane, 2002, p. 1).

WHAT CAN SLOW THE PROGRESSION?

In the travel industry, the tragedy of 9/11 slowed the progression, not just online, but with all travel sales. It's difficult to predict what would have happened in travel if our nation had not been attacked. Travel companies had less money to invest because fewer people traveled, and this slowed the progression of technology a bit.

The real estate sector has enjoyed tremendously low interest rates, propelling growth into double-digit numbers in most areas throughout the country. As interest rates increase under the federal current monetary policy and business slows, we can expect organizations to begin investing in technology that will make it cheaper and faster for them to do business, while limiting the amount of staff required for a transaction. Staff almost always costs more than technology, that is, after the technology is implemented.

This all leads to even more online purchasing and less hand-holding, not a good sign for real estate professionals or mortgage brokers in particular. We can also expect consumers to be more wary, and potentially in the short term to turn to traditional methods of buying and selling, although a weakening market (if it happens) is the worst reason to do so. The goal is to get the most money out of the transaction as a seller, and using an agent in a traditional model doesn't do this for them. You must either create a niche for yourself in which your cost is lower than your value by adding value or lowering your cost, or you must find a completely different way to revamp your business and compete. Later in the book, I will offer specific suggestions. A warning to those of you who are still using traditional techniques to sell your service: Sellers are not nearly as into "warm fuzzy feelings" as they used to be simply because the cost of that feeling is too great.

WREAKING HAVOC ON ADVERTISING

To thoroughly examine the way technology is impacting real estate, we should look at the ways that traditional real estate professionals advertise the homes and sellers they are representing. By looking at the impact the Internet has had on complementary goods of traditional real estate sales, we can understand a bit more of the trend occurring in the industry. One of these complementary goods is print media, a popular method by which agents or agencies often advertise homes they have listed for sale. A report by Borrell Asssociates Inc. notes that the Internet is significantly eroding newspaper advertising for real estate. This trend will continue, based on the spread and integration of technology and the possibilities for the future. Why is this important? Because it indicates that agents are turning to the Internet for listing homes and that for-sale-by-owner clients are not using traditional mechanisms to advertise their houses.

The Internet Data Exchange (IDX) broker permission-based consumer access to MLS listings allows consumers to access MLS databases that are "roughly 15 times more comprehensive than newspaper or home magazine classifieds or display ads," according to a report in *Realty Times* titled "New Report Shows Internet Eroding Newspaper Real Estate Advertising" (Evans, 2005, p. 1). Agents have adopted the Internet era where it helps them: advertising. But as a group of professionals, you have yet to see the true impact of what is occurring. According to the 2004 update, "Online Real Estate Advertising Comes of Age," a report written for suburban newspapers in America:

- In 1996, agents, brokers, and developers spent $755 on newspaper advertising for every single home sold. This decreased in 2004 to $605 per home.
- Online spending per home increased from $14 to $148 during the same time period. This means that agents realize people are using the Internet to find homes.
- Newspapers and home magazines received 70 percent of all real estate advertising spending in the mid-1990s. As we know, newspaper circulation and production rates are down thanks to Internet news media. However, even knowing circulation is down and accounting for this, newspaper erosion hasn't kept pace with housing sales that are increasing while newspapers and home magazines are receiving fewer listings.

THE INTERNET AND MLS

The MLS is the lifeblood of communicating available homes to consumers and agents. According to MediaMatrix in July 2004, brokerage companies occupy 9 of the top 20 spots on the Internet in terms of totals for unique visitors. It's important to note that a unique visitor is not a calculation of "Web site hits," which is not a good indicator of the usefulness of the Web site, but actually the unique times an individual visits the site, which is a very good indicator of its true usage.

A transition is taking place in the MLS industry. After surveying 30 MLS executives in the United States (representing 18 percent of the 2.1 million MLS listings), Borrell Associates noted that listing services have shifted from publishing listings data to facilitating the delivery of listings electronically to brokers' and agents' Web sites, thus directly publishing data from the MLS to a particular agent or agency Web site. While this sounds good, it is simply prolonging the use of the middleman and shows that real estate agents are playing catch-up with today's technology rather than planning for the future. You want to plan for the future and create something for your client that is greater than regurgitation of information they can get elsewhere.

Worse yet for the real estate industry, the study found that 53 percent of MLSs offer available listings directly to the public. They may charge a small fee, but the information is available. Thus you need not go to your hometown agent's web site to find out what is available online. Those of you with *www.realtorjoesmith.com* are wasting your time putting up MLS listings when big companies offer entire national markets on their sites.

So who's top in the online market? The study found that 97 percent of listing services (MLSs) provide listings to REAL-TOR.com, while only 27 percent provided them to local newspapers. Again this indicates a movement away from traditional advertising to Web-based dynamic searching and acquisition capabilities because those responsible for advertising know that folks are looking online. In addition, this is a breakthrough for REALTOR.com. One of the "rules" of the trade is that you can only buy an MLS for an area you are licensed in. This creates difficulty for companies that want to sell properties throughout the country but are only licensed in one area or one state, if they're lucky. REALTOR.com has partnered with agents to be able to provide MLS listings for nearly 100 percent of the market, creating a huge capability for them and truly providing value. Real estate professionals take note! Once again, the strong will survive—you can use this as a tool rather than trying to compete with it.

Less than 17 percent of listing services receive money for listings. Some will give their data away for free (particularly in areas that want to showcase their properties because of their distance from popular home sale areas), and others will charge the agencies or agents up-front fees to obtain MLS feeds.

Almost $11.5 billion was spent in 2004 by real estate advertisers to reach potential buyers, sellers, apartment renters, etc. This decreased from 2003, when 11.2 percent of this money was spent online and 40 percent of this was allocated to newspapers. One of the keys in this finding is that apartment renters were lumped into the group, a market that hasn't made the transition to online advertising as quickly or thoroughly as the buying and selling of real property has. Expect this number to begin shifting dramatically as the rental markets catch up with the sales markets.

In 2004, newspapers lost 6.1 percent of print real estate revenue, but made up 43 percent of the 6.1 percent loss with their online operations. What does this tell you? There's an old saying in real estate investing that you should "Start building where Home Depot does." In other words, the marketing department of Home Depot is far greater and better than what an investor alone can study, so follow its lead. The study does not indicate whether the makeup of income is coming directly from advertising for real estate or by all online activities, so the number becomes hard to correlate to a particular trend, though the number itself is of interest.

Newspapers receive 94 percent of their online revenues from listings or listing enhancements; however, the trend in this business is to move away from charging for the listings and instead toward lead generation and paid searches, much like the big online companies do. Again, this is another lead you could follow.

Newspaper general managers who were surveyed by this organization note that the greatest competitors to their newspapers online are their own customers, the agents and brokers, and specifically list REALTOR.com.

A spokesman and author of the report for Borrell Associates notes that agents are moving toward spending their advertising dollars online. This follows a trend we already know has a stronghold on the market.

Interestingly enough, the study found that the Internet ranks number two—only behind the yard sign—in reaching the potential buyer, and 75 percent of the public uses the Internet in their home searches. Many of these potential buyers are bringing lists of the homes they want to see to their agent because there is no cost to them and it's convenient to have the buyer's agent set up the showing. Another potential niche market if you are paying attention!

You've probably noticed (and we'll discuss this in much greater detail) that many of the sites will lead you to homes by searching many MLSs simultaneously and then refer you to an agent. Many of these companies, such as Housevalues and Homestore, are generating substantial profits simply from lead generation. In the future, neither will be necessary because the consumer will simply be able to purchase the property, fill out paperwork, send in necessary deposits, and secure a lender and an escrow company all online, seamlessly and transparently.

ONLINE REAL ESTATE SALES

According to ZDNet Research, the top real estate sites online are REALTOR.com, HomeGain, and AOL Real Estate. AOL has two things going for it: market share and marketing. Its management teams have been smart enough to move into markets they see having great online potential. Much like investors follow home-improvement stores or Wal-Marts, many technologists follow AOL's acquisitions and value-added services to understand where the market is headed.

Nielsen//NetRatings reported that continued interest in home and rental properties created a market of 21.6 million Web surfers, 15 percent of the *active* Internet population, who visited a real estate site or an apartment rental site in April 2005. This is an increase of 26 percent during a similar test taken just six months prior. The same type of findings were reported early in the booming online travel industry, yet another reason to draw conclusions that the industries share the same fate.

When looking strictly at the top 10 real estate and apartment sites, they collectively grew in visitors from 8.2 million in November 2004 to 12.6 million in April 2005, which is an astounding 54 percent increase. Many say this is simply a reflection of the booming real estate market; but did the real estate market grow

54 percent in this time frame? Demand for these sites is still increasing at astounding rates even while interest rates climb.

WHO'S ON TOP IN ONLINE REAL ESTATE?

In April 2005, REALTOR.com had more than 2 million listings on its site, bringing the largest audience of all online real estate companies to its business. This generated 6 million *different* visitors to the site. Some companies when reporting their Web statistics refer to "hits," or the number of times a page is requested. If the same person hits the page 20 times, that is 20 hits, which isn't an accurate representation of visitation. REALTOR.com properly reported its information as *visitors,* and unique ones at that. Despite being in the real estate industry, these types of numbers would make most online companies envious. Being in the real estate industry just makes them even more profound. They offer the great benefit of being able to search almost every single MLS from one site.

The second most visited site is HomeGain, which had more than 3 million unique visitors in one month, again in April 2005. In fact, HomeGain issued a press release years ago in October 2000. In 2005, those six-month numbers were climbing 83 percent. HomeGain's research indicated that sellers who use the Internet to sell report higher sales prices than those using traditional means. In fact, for the months of June through August 2000, the average seller sold his or her home for over 15 percent more by using online methods over traditional ones.

The National Association of Realtors® (NAR) reported that at least for one test area, that particular summer yielded an online average sales price of $207,713 compared to $179,466 for offline sales. As a professor of statistics, I must point out that many variables may be impacting this. Perhaps those online simply had more money (and could afford Internet access) and, therefore, lived in nicer houses. The association did not report the actual statistics so I could not run analyses myself, but this is something to think about. It should also be pointed out that most online companies such as HomeGain will also help consumers find an agent to represent them, one they claim caters to the more educated and higher-income "Internet buyer," although numbers to prove or disprove this claim haven't been reported. If this holds true for the future (and I believe it will), then this is just another reason for consumers to avoid using real estate professionals.

AOL reported 3 million prospective buyers or renters visited its site in 2005. This was 26 percent in just 6 months, according to Nielsen//NetRatings. Since most people who don't subscribe to AOL don't visit its site regularly, it's safe to assume most of these 3 million visitors were AOL subscribers. As AOL loses market share as many technologists are predicting, these numbers may shift and either be absorbed by a new third-place company or transition to one of the other two companies, or yet another one altogether.

Although counterintuitive, lower income households in mid-2005 were reported to be the fastest growing group of online real estate site visitors.

According to Nielsen//NetRatings in May 2005, Table 3.1 represents the site and its unique audience.

TABLE 3.1 *Six-month Growth of Top Ten Sites*

SITE	APRIL 2005 UNIQUE AUDIENCE	NOVEMBER 2004 UNIQUE AUDIENCE	SIX-MONTH GROWTH
Site	5,753,000	4,270,000	35%
REALTOR.com	3,133,000	2,356,000	33%
HomeGain	2,670,000	855,000	212%
AOL Real Estate	1,515,000	782,000	94%
RealtyTrac	1,366,000	733,000	86%
Rent.com	1,320,000	806,000	64%
Yahoo! Real Estate	1,132,000	604,000	87%
Century 21	990,000	409,000	142%
ForSaleByOwner.com	893,000	628,000	42%
RealEstate.com	890,000	603,000	48%
RENTNET	5,753,000	4,270,000	35%

Source: Nielsen//NetRatings, May 2005

These numbers are astounding! The Web site *www.allNSabout-marketresearch.com* offers a tremendous amount of information on this topic, and you should spend some time with the numbers.

According to the site (see Table 3.2), "Nielsen//NetRatings reported an overall jump in visitors from all income brackets to real estate and apartment sites during April of 2005. Lower-income households earning up to $25K showed the most significant growth with a million potential homebuyers and renters viewing a real estate or apartment site last month, marking a 47 percent leap during the past six months."

THE FSBO MARKET

In mid-2005, ForSaleByOwner.com drew nearly a million unique visitors, jumping 142 percent from six months prior, according to Nielsen//NetRatings, suggesting consumers are taking homeselling into their own hands. This trend is catching on because it's quite easy for the consumer—and cheaper. For-sale-by-owner markets are making up a larger portion of home sales in the United States than ever before. This is almost entirely because the Internet has made it easier to do and the average consumer has access to list his or her home in the MLS, a benefit held only by real estate professionals in the past. The market leader in for-sale-by-owner sales is ForSaleByOwner.com. In the same month,

TABLE 3.2 *FSix-month Growth According to Income*

Household Income	April 2005 Unique Audience	Six-month Growth
$0–24,999	1,000,000	47%
$50,000–74,999	6,179,000	32%
$150,000+	2,254,000	29%
$75,000–99,999	3,983,000	24%
$100,000–149,999	3,919,000	22%
$25,000–49,999	3,966,000	20%

Source: Nielsen//NetRatings, May 2005

reporting for the other market leaders, this site drew more than 1 million visitors, a 142 percent jump over six months prior. This incredible increase is a signal that as the process becomes easier and the various steps involved in real estate transaction look more like a commodity, buyers and sellers may be taking matters into their own hands. This is great for sellers, but bad for real estate professionals.

Homebuyers, especially investors, are finding there is simply nothing to be afraid of, unless they are in a really, really unique position. Most online for-sale-by-owner sites will walk consumers through the process, provide yard signs, help list a home on the MLS, provide the opportunity to post and list numerous pictures, and even create a link to a virtual tour that sellers create themselves using their home video camera. In fact, I found out first-hand how terrific some for-sale-by-owner sites can be by selling my home this way; they provided flyers to print out, allowed multiple picture uploads, told me where to get a lockbox and where to document the combination, and offered helpful suggestions on holding an open house. I sold one house in two days, and the other in two weeks.

4

KNOW YOUR COMPETITION

Today, the average homebuyer or homeseller has incredible tools available that will help him or her through the entire process of buying and selling homes online, including securing mortgages, finding and listing homes, and setting up times to visit the home. The average homebuyer can use the Internet to maximize profits, simplify the process, and make wise choices. Many methods and even more tools are available for this practice, and this holds true for investors too (perhaps even more so). To understand what your clientele thinks and to successfully market and sell to them, you must understand what it is they have at their disposal. In this chapter we will explore the tools available to the average consumer that lets him or her use the Internet like a pro.

MAPPING SOFTWARE

Mapping software has revolutionized the way we look at demographics and has provided visuals on areas a buyer may purchase in. As we discussed earlier in this book, overlays are possible that will show consumers the location of gas stations, airports, highways (even those intended but not built), air force bases, etc. This helps consumers assess the possibility of noise, crime, traffic, etc., in an area before they even begin to look for a home. Alternatively, they can look up the home after finding something of interest to see if it fits the demographics they are looking for: good schools, the right-size population, available shopping, or quick access to freeways. This is all information that at one point area specialists and real estate agents were able to provide; in fact, it was one of the only ways of getting it, short of doing a lot of research at a local library. In fact, even many of the online realty companies provide a snapshot of demographics immediately, including crime (and crime compared to the national average), population data, average income, rating of the school system, etc. Whatever anyone wants to know, he or she will be able to find it with the use of a small tool chest of online applications.

MAPPING AND ONLINE IMAGING

Satellite imaging has taken off like a rocket. Take, for instance, Google Earth. Google Earth is an incredible tool that shows satellite images of just about any area on earth. Now many sites such as Zillow.com are incorporating Google Earth–like images into their comps! Zillow's goal is to get "zillions of data points" out there to the consumer (Zillow, 2006)! If you haven't seen this site, you need to immediately. The power it brings to the consumer in my opinion is second to none. This is yet another source that will be a hot option in the future for your consumers to find good data. Google is actively mapping the world, and while some images are a little outdated, it can get a closeup of a particular property or see an area in general, as well as overlay many of the infrastructure components of a particular area to see where a property resides in relation to these conveniences (or inconveniences). Available at *earth.google.com*, this requires a small download from a reputable company, yet pays huge dividends to your clients. This is especially helpful if the consumer is moving into a new area or purchasing investment property that he or she may not have time to view before closing the deal. If the consumer is searching for even greater detailed property and neighborhood specific information, he or she may choose to check out *maps.a9.com*. While the site doesn't have every neighborhood (or even close to it) as of the date this book was written, the information it does have is astounding and provides panoramic and tour-like views of various areas.

The e-Neighborhoods site provides data on just about any neighborhood a consumer may choose to purchase in.

REFERENCES AND RESOURCES

In today's world, it is sometimes difficult to know who to trust. Some individuals online have created documents for consumers to determine who to trust and who not to trust. For instance, a link of Yahoo at *http://loan.yahoo.com/m/cq_refer.html* asks the question, "I am anxious about getting a mortgage because everybody wants to make money from me. How do I know who I can trust?" Specifically, the author of the article talks about how to know which referrals to trust and which ones not to trust. This is a great example of information your consumers are using to determine whether or not to trust you—most likely, you didn't know it even existed.

Let's look at some examples mentioned at the site Real Estate Sales. "Home purchasers accept more referrals from real estate sales agents than from all other sources combined. The home-buyer often establishes a relationship with the agent during the house-hunting phase, and the agent is there when the need for a mortgage arises. Sales agents have the same interest as buyers in getting deals done. Hence, they refer clients to loan providers who can generally be depended upon to close on time. Sales agents have no comparable interest in the mortgage price, and are not concerned if the price is a little above the market. However, the agent doesn't want the price to be so far out of line that the borrower throws a fit and blames the agent. Loan providers spend a lot of time cultivating the favor of sales agents. The law prohibits paying for referrals, but it is not enforceable and violations occur—how frequently, nobody knows. I would much prefer a referral from an agent who doesn't get paid by the loan provider."

Note the type of information your own clients are getting that you may not even know about. This quoted author is telling clients how to know if your opinion is reputable or not! Let's look at another and continue quoting:

> Some borrowers seek the comfort of a trusted name as their loan provider. Their logic is that a lender with a reputation to protect is not going to jeopardize it by overcharging borrowers. There is some but not much merit in this approach. Some name lenders systematically price above the market. Their policy is that borrowers should pay for the comfort of dealing with them. In addition, the loan officers employed by these lenders have some discretion in pricing loans. If the loan officer tabs you as unknowledgeable and timid, you will probably pay an "overage"—a price above the price listed on the loan officer's price sheet. The lender and the loan officer usually share overages. If you are smart and forceful, on the other hand, you might get an underage—a price below the listed price. There are many more overages than underages. On the other hand, name lenders cap the size of overages. Although you may pay too much dealing with a name lender, the overpayment won't be outrageous.

DEMOGRAPHICS

There are lots of places where consumers can pull up true demographic data. They can start with the Web site of the county they are looking to move to or purchase property in. Usually, companies or organizations publish demographic data and the job or economic outlook in the area. A consumer site that can't be overlooked despite its longevity in the market is Mapquest at *www.mapquest.com*. The site provides an incredible information-rich presentation and useful data for your potential clients to use to make knowledgeable decisions. They can simply query a search engine such as *www.google.com* as well, and type in keywords such as "demographics Austin" to pull up demographic data on that particular market. Also take some time to explore *www.terraxsite.com* for additional information, which is distributed by the *Real Estate Journal.*

Another way to pull up demographic data is by zip code. Often this provides more specific information than simply by typing in the city name, which we know has its good and bad areas. Zip codes are more specific and tend to be drawn around economic boundaries as well (which came first, the zip code or the income?). Check out *library.csun.edu/mfinley/zipstats.html*.

Another fascinating site with information on demographics is Melissa Data, at *www.melissadata.com/Lookups/*. This lets consumers search more than 30 databases for information that they want! Try it yourself and you will see why you are being asked fewer questions about demographics these days and are dealing with a far more educated consumer base.

ESRI has also integrated business statistics into its consumer Web site. ESRI in Redlands, California, long known for its incredible Geographical Information Systems and world-renowned software, has a consumer site that offers incredible information. It used to be popular only in the health care market, but as you'll see by visiting the site, this is no longer the case. You can locate the site at *www.esri.com*.

MORTGAGE CALCULATORS AND INTEREST-RATE COMPARISON TOOLS

Without a long-term relationship with an honest banker, I can't for the life of me imagine why someone would consider purchasing an investment property or residence without looking into what banks in their area are offering for interest rates. I'm sure as a real estate professional, you can't, either. Individual banks only offer *their* interest rates on loans, not their competitors' rates. A few years ago, rate comparison companies such as LendingTree started their own niche; let banks compete for your business. Even LendingTree only works with some banks. If this doesn't sound like the start of a commodity market, I don't know what does! Lendingtree.com is a good place to start if a consumer is serious about receiving bids right away. And eLoan.com is another site considered reputable by consumers.

To begin researching what your consumers have at their fingertips, start with a simple and easy site and look at the incredible information-rich data. Look at Yahoo's Finance section on Mortgages at *finance.yahoo.com/loan/mortgage*.

If a consumer just wants to know what the mortgage rates are today, he or she can check out *www.bankrate.com*, which provides a world of information on this subject, a tool to calculate how much home a person can afford, and information on who has the cheapest loans in an area (can you say commodity?). Consumers can also check their favorite search engine for other providers of such handy (and cost-saving) information. The Mortgage Professor provides a variety of spreadsheets for the consumers to compare various mortgages and offers at *www.mtgprofessor.com/spreadsheets.htm*. When you visit this site, you will be amazed at the volume of spreadsheets that Jack Guttentag has had on the Internet for years!

Remember that when a consumer receives a good-faith estimate from a bank, it's acceptable to scrutinize it and ask for reductions, particularly if the consumer is using a broker. Personally, I have never recommended that any friends use brokers unless my friends had bad credit, or I had a friend in the business I knew would not upcharge much and my friends or colleagues would come out ahead. Part of the reason for this is the data and information from credible sources I have received on the Internet and my ability to compare loan rates immediately.

The key for consumers these days is to be educated. Because real estate professionals can't stop this natural evolution, it's better to accommodate for it rather than fight it; better yet, be a part of it!

For example, a highly educated banker who I consider a friend tried to convince me why I shouldn't go with a negative amortization loan on my primary residence, but the truth is his bank simply didn't offer it. I didn't know that at first—and this gentleman was a friend! Looking online, I found that while his competition offered such a loan, his bank did not. He was simply serving himself when he advised me, and, of course, I don't blame him. When he changed banks and went to work for one that did offer that type of loan, suddenly it was the best thing since sliced bread. Consumers should understand that banks, and especially brokers, are looking out for themselves in most cases. They are realizing that the real estate business is just like any other business and making money is the primary goal.

This is especially true for brokers, who, in general, receive a bad name particularly in the investment community. Banks who do offer various loan programs will push one or the other because loan officers tend to make more money on different types of loans, and negative amortization is one that is hot. This allows an individual to buy a house he or she could otherwise not afford, and lets the bank tack on more interest, possibly prepayment penalties, and other negatives. Sometimes these loans make it difficult to obtain an equity line or a second mortgage, so consumers are beginning to watch out for these instruments, particularly if a broker is trying to sell a loan. Regardless of what area of real estate you are in, know your market and know what your partners are offering to your clients.

COMPARATIVE MARKET ANALYSIS

In my opinion, this one tool, the comparative analysis online, has singlehandedly pierced the veil of protection real estate professionals once enjoyed. Just wait until Generation Y starts investing! The key to comps is to find out what other homes in a neighborhood with similar square footage have sold for. As mentioned earlier, Zillow.com is a pioneer in this area, but it is still in beta at the time this book was sent to print. This important number used in appraisals will determine not only what the consumer should expect to sell for and act as a starting point for a listing price, but will be the basis for what banks are willing to lend buyers. This also gives a consumer good leverage if he or she decides to use an agent to represent the sale, because he or she will be an educated consumer and won't be roped into traditional tactics.

This is important to sellers because many loans have appraisal and loan contingencies, meaning the buyer can back out of the deal with no financial loss if the home doesn't appraise at the purchase price or if the buyer can't get a loan, again depending on the appraisal. Although many buyers will simply ask a seller to re-negotiate the price if a home doesn't appraise high enough, some will use this as an excuse to back out of a deal, costing the seller precious time and money. In addition, contingencies mean they may have to give the earnest money back, again benefiting the buyer. Pricing a home is also critical to selling it quickly and attracting buyers fast. If you want to look up these analyses, check out *www.homeseekers.com* and *www.domania.com*. Zillow also offers free price analyses online.

HomePriceCheck at *www.homepricecheck.com* has been advertising more lately to try out its valuing services, though some don't give the data right away and ask the visitor to fill out a form for an agent to contact them. I *strongly* advise that individuals stay away from this and you should advise your clients to do the same. This is a marketing ploy and, honestly, those of us in technology don't want anything to do with it. You're better off showing your value, not tricking consumers. Of these sites, Domania is by far my favorite. To date, I haven't received any unsolicited e-mail (that I'm aware of) from this company by using its tools. This doesn't mean it doesn't use Spyware, but I haven't analyzed its site to find out. Zillow also hasn't sent any unsolicited e-mail, so it may be a good one to send your clients to. Two other tools are *www.valueyourhome. realestatejournal.com* and *www.domania.com/index.jsp*.

SURVEY SAYS?

To really explain what's going on in the market, I thought it was important to understand what those of you in the profession think and feel about the changes. While preparing to present on the impact of technology on the real estate profession at an international symposium in China, a colleague, Dr. Alex Lazo, and I studied the effects of IT on the real estate industry from a unique perspective—from that of the same professionals who are potentially impacted. A group of e-mail addresses was collected and these real estate agents were sent e-mails explaining that a research study was being conducted on the impact of technology on their profession. Given that the survey was Web-based, any statistician will tell you that it has some internal bias and that it has lower than desirable response rates, but it is a good starting point and provides an interesting look at the situation.

So what did those of you surveyed have to say? Well, let me first explain what we asked them. The questions asked were related to the following topics:

- How technology has changed the real estate business
- The threat perceived by technology to the business
- The potential business opportunity provided by technology
- The degree to which professionals surveyed are taking advantage of the technology
- Whether his or her business is working with a technology partner

- The overall impact on his or her business and any general comments on the topic.

Question 1: How much has technology changed the real estate business of buying and selling residential property (single-family residence, duplex, triplex, fourplex)?

An overwhelming 92 percent of the respondents believe technology has changed the real estate business "moderately" to "a lot." Some 8 percent of the respondents chose "some," and zero respondents chose very little. This clearly indicates that real estate professionals believe that technology has changed the way they do business. About 80 percent of those respondents believe that change is characterized as "a lot." So, clearly, they understand that technology is having an impact. But what are they doing about it?

Question 2: Do you feel technology threatens the way you traditionally do business?

About 86 percent of the respondents do not feel that technology threatens the way they traditionally do business. A more intuitive or perhaps more educated 14 percent believes it does. The responses to this question were a bit odd, given the statements made in the comments section about having to meet increasing client needs. The qualitative data indicate that these same agents believe they can maximize their use of the Internet rather than compete with it. To find a way to do this, they will need to find value to add above and beyond what can occur by simply clicking on a property to purchase and following through with the transaction online. They will need to become a Nordstrom or a Barnes & Noble, get creative, and consistently add value where it currently is not being added.

Question 3: Do you feel the Internet has created opportunity for you?

Approximately 97 percent of the respondents said yes; 3 percent said no. Clearly, those saying yes (based on qualitative data or the comments section) believe they can use the Internet to show property pictures, e-mail their clients, and communicate faster with their potential buyers and sellers. No doubt, this has created opportunity for them where it did not exist before. The Internet has provided them with a greater base of clientele, more visibility, and faster leads. As the future changes and electronic systems becomes more "intelligent," however, professionals will need to find their niche all over again, or the agents' services will simply become a commodity, with online companies providing it faster and cheaper.

Question 4: How much are you currently taking advantage of technology to increase your sales, decrease your sales cycle, and increase your revenue?

Surprisingly, only 70 percent of respondents are taking advantage of technology, while 17 percent are taking some advantage. This means that they may be using some technologies to help them be more efficient, provide listings or some particular services, but they are not taking full advantage of technology in their opinions. Keep in mind that this is only the technology available today! The rest are not taking advantage at all. The responses to this question were quite surprising, given that most of the technology is available free or at a very inexpensive rate to agents if they choose to use it. Most worrisome is that many real estate professionals aren't thinking of the future, only the here and now. Technology changes rapidly and they need to be one step ahead of the game.

Question 5: Are you working with a technology organization to make sure you and/or your business are conducting transactions using technology in the most efficient way?

The results to this question were mixed: 75 percent of the respondents are working "a lot," a "moderate" amount, or "some" with a technology organization. About 25 percent are not using the expertise that a company can offer them to help them maintain an advantage in today's Internet-savvy market. Again, this is concerting; if the Internet revolutionizes the real estate market as it has other markets, these same professionals will be in for an unwelcome surprise in a decade or less.

Question 6: Overall, would you say the impact technology is having on your business is "a lot," "a moderate amount," "some," "a little," or "not at all"?

A little over 85 percent of the respondents indicated that technology is having "a lot" to "a moderate" impact on their business, yet only 75 percent of them are working with technology companies. This disjointed figure is going to be the downfall of many of these professionals who are left wondering how several clicks on a Web page replaced them. If a fourth of these respondents aren't working with technologists for today's technology, how in the world will they keep up with what tomorrow is going to bring?

Finally, some of the comments collected include:

- Buyers are coming into the process more educated than before.
- Sellers are comparing commissions more often and choosing who costs less rather than taking into consideration the agent's experience.
- Buyers often have a list of homes they are interested in prior to ever calling an agent.
- Clients require less face time and more online communications.
- Communication is better and easier with clients.
- There is a paperwork reduction, but often more time is spent figuring out the technology.
- Sending properties for clients to review is far easier than before the Internet.
- The Internet has increased the value of what agents are offering.
- It is easier to market to people outside of an agent's area.
- Technology has had a permanent impact on the way we do business.
- We can do more in the same amount of time.
- Technology is underused by clients because they could find out more about agents' credentials.

- Having pictures online makes things easier for all parties involved.

SUMMARIZING THE FINDINGS

So how can we summarize all these findings? Rather simply, actually. First, real estate professionals in most cases do not understand the long-term impact of technology on their business. They appear to take a naive approach to the Internet, seeing it as a tool to help do work faster and better, which may be the case today but not necessarily in the future. The future will hold a tighter grip on the market, allowing buyers and sellers to virtually complete the entire transaction without any real estate agent hands-on involvement whatsoever. We are already seeing a significant shift in the amount of homes for sale by owner. The individual who noted that consumers are underutilizing the Internet was probably most accurate in his or her assessment.

As this gets easier, why will sellers pay relatively high fees when they can do it themselves? Right now, the information you hold and the fear that advertisements have caused ("You can't possibly do this without a professional, it's so complicated," etc.) are keeping an invisible wall around you. In addition to the ease of transactions that will occur when transaction-based processing finally touches real estate completely, the transparency of information once held tightly will erode one of the perceived benefits of real estate professionals.

Eventually, as with other markets, information leads to transparency and transparency leads to the legitimization of an industry in an electronic form, and the wall once built will disappear. The opinions of most of those polled, given the outlook on the industry and a look at the history of Web technology, appear shortsighted and do not take into consideration the enormous potential the Internet has to threaten their business entirely. Some may blame the organizations designed to protect them for not looking out for their interests; others may blame the professionals themselves for not researching the tools being developed and deployed like wildfire. While you have enjoyed technology that has enabled your business to run better and has given you additional tools, you will find yourselves soon competing with the very technology you embraced. It's imperative you take action now to consider new business strategies for positioning in the future.

Another easy conclusion to make is that some, although very few, really do get it. Some do feel their business is threatened, not enhanced, by the Internet. This is the correct thinking; an entire paradigm shift must occur for you to have a place in the future market. This will require creativity and unique approaches to an age-old problem that is starting to hit the real estate profession. The Internet is known for breaking down the middleman. eBay has created the "perfect market"; buyers and sellers can connect directly while everyone pays less fees. Not to mention sellers' markets have became global literally overnight. Why will this same phenomenon not hit real estate?

Some agents are correct. Today, communicating with pictures online, creating virtual tours that "only my company can do right and post immediately," and showing your home via data from the MLS as well as the combination to the lockbox on a house is important. But what if sellers and buyers could do these things themselves? What if they could register for lockbox combinations? What if agents weren't needed at all? What if for a small fee, a consumer could pay someone just to let others into his or her house and watch potential buyers to make sure they don't steal anything and answer simple questions—for far less than 5 percent to 6 percent commission? Most of these technologies and services are available today, and many of us have used them successfully. What about tomorrow when technology is an even greater threat to the industry than it is now?

NEXT STEPS FOR REAL ESTATE PROFESSIONALS

So what should you, as a real estate professional, do about all of this? An entire chapter is devoted to this, exploring other industries and how successful ones have navigated the Internet storm. A first step is recognition and the realization that the Internet may not be a good thing for your business. We must consider the history of technology and how the Web has transformed some industries, albeit many slower than others. Then we must consider environmental or generational differences in the population, taking into consideration that the cohort growing up with an incredible and often misunderstood comfort with online transactions will feel secure enough to do this on their own or with little guidance, and, thus, little commission.

You must find a way to add value for your clients with out-of-the-box thinking, not just additional Internet pictures and an e-mail address that you check when you think about it. I am reminded of an experience with an agent recently where I was selling a property, a secondary residence, in an area I don't live in. The agent never phoned or e-mailed, and the only way to get a response from her was to call her manager. This is not the way to do business—ever—much less in an Internet age where it is expected you are available during office hours (and beyond) from anywhere you might be. Use what services are available today and use them to their fullest. Be known as the person with the "greatest and latest" technology, so that when it changes drastically you already have a great reputation. Start networking now with those organizations that are expected to be stars in the next generation of the Web. Realize that word of mouth is still important, but consider new ways that word of mouth is being heard: blogging, news groups, etc. These are all valid forms of communication and are virtually ignored by real estate professionals.

Embrace technologies, but hire experts who may be able to help you stay one step ahead of what is being released. Remain one step ahead of the curve rather than behind it by predicting where technology is leading the industry and then successfully strategizing to be there when it happens. Be prepared today for what is in store tomorrow; consider high-bandwidth requirements and storage capabilities, look at real ways to add value by reviewing other successful industries, consider true development, and conduct research. Build infrastructure, and search—be prepared, see what your clients see.

TECHNOLOGIES FOR CONSIDERATION TODAY—AVAILABLE NOW

There are several technologies that you don't need to wait for tomorrow to implement. We can be proactive and implement some today, and then be prepared for what tomorrow will bring.

Technologies available today provide numerous opportunities, including those presented by customer relationship management (CRM) applications, listing services, automatic generation of investment property data, sales-tracking solutions, and, most important, communication technologies. Some things you may consider doing immediately include:

- Talk to people who aren't your clients using a blog or another forum to find out why they aren't working with you and embrace "anywhere" technologies like instant messaging and phone messaging. Implement sales-tracking tools that will help you manage your sales funnel, and prepare to enhance your Web site dramatically with the ability to not only search MLSs, but to download data sheets that are enhanced significantly with cash-flow analyses, payment calculations, etc.
- Partner with those who provide online tools such as mortgage calculators and build that into your Web site—not a link but actual data on your Web page. Make your page a one-stop shop and add value by means of streamlining information.

- Understand the client's preferences in the face of a new market. If your client e-mails you, respond by e-mail. Don't phone a client who is obviously attempting to communicate with you in the written form unless you are asked to do so.
- Read books on using the Internet and how to build Web pages and update your systems frequently. This will at least keep you current with what's out there and what your competitors are doing now; in the meantime, we'll try to prepare you for what's coming.
- Provide value-added services online within your own Web page, such as bank-rate calculators, loan comparisons, appreciation rates, or anything else that is important to an investor or someone purchasing a primary residence. Try not to resist the trend toward a more educated consumer.
- Most of all, try to grasp the difference between Web enabled and Web based. There is a big difference and that will be the primary underlying reason the real estate industry will change so dramatically in the coming years. Web-enable today, but prepare your business for a Web-*based* world tomorrow.

This is only the beginning, and it's the basics. It really is what you already should have done, but maybe haven't quite gotten to yet. Chapter 6 on what you can do about it now to prepare for the future will help provide more detailed information on how to specifically do this by reviewing other industries, taking an inside look at the motivation of information technologists, understanding where the Web came from and where it's going, and analyzing those who have successfully navigated similar transitions within their own industries. We have as much to learn from those who have made the transition well as we do from those who haven't;— and we'll explore both.

ONLINE MARKETING

According to Payam Zamani, CEO of Next Phase Media Inc., "72 percent of all salespeople and brokers who responded [to a survey] said they need an online marketing program." Again, this reflects a complete misunderstanding of the future. This may be what is needed today, but to survive (or better yet, flourish), it's going to take a lot more than an online marketing program to sustain sales—that's not to say you shouldn't start there. It's going to take an entire paradigm shift in thinking about the way sales transactions are handled. The survey conducted by Next Phase, which provides leads to agents, surveyed 10,000 real estate salespeople and brokers. The survey yielded a very low response rate (about 2.1 percent), which may indicate invalid results. Or it may mean that the professionals didn't have updated e-mail addresses, didn't know how to use the online survey system, wouldn't take the time to respond, or simply doesn't check their e-mail addresses very often. Not one of these explanations for the low response rate is good for the industry.

Regardless of the response rate, assuming it's representative of the population, let's look at the makeup of the individuals who responded:

- 63.4 percent were salespeople (it wasn't specified what type of salespeople, and if their primary clients were investors or homeowners).
- 36.6 percent were brokers (again it was not specified if they are real estate brokers or mortgage brokers).
- 34.8 percent said they had more than 15 years of experience, but experience isn't defined.
- 65.2 percent were affiliated with a real estate brokerage.
- 30.9 percent said they were independent, or working on their own, and not affiliated with an agency or brokerage.
- Most said they are bullish on their respective markets, with 21.9 percent expecting a very strong sales year and 42.8 percent expecting a strong sales year.

The survey contained 21 questions, rating marketing tools on a scale of 1 to 5, with 1 indicating the most effective tool and 5 indicating the least effective tool. The results were interesting, given the move toward an Internet-based model, signifying the change will shock more than not:

- 51 percent cited the "for sale" sign in front of the home as the most effective lead-generation tool.
- In second place was an Internet Web presence at 29 percent.
- Open houses and direct marketing ranked third, each scoring in first place by 20 percent of the respondents.

Most interesting, given my own primary research, were questions about how the Internet has impacted their business. A little over 71 percent indicated that an Internet campaign is critical to remaining at the top of their market, and 28.6 percent provides MLS on their Web sites, leading to new clients. (It's important to note that an agent cannot pull MLS data if he or she isn't licensed in a particular state or area, so the MLS listings on individual sites are highly incomplete at best.) This is where giants such as REALTOR.com come in and truly add value.

WHAT DOES ALL THIS TELL US?

The data collected from the trends in other industries, the opinions and the attitudes of real estate professionals, all tell us that the future markets aren't in line with the opinions and choices of professionals in the industry. There may be many new niches real estate professionals choose to enter, or even new markets to create. Rather than wasting valuable time figuring out why you aren't prepared, let's work on preparing you.

New niches are everywhere and lots of possibilities exist. For instance, perhaps you will handle the sale of an investor's home while he or she is not in the area, a valuable service that may continue well into the future, especially as more people look to real estate as their primary investment tool. Another potential is the existing model, but at significantly reduced rates. I liken this to the supermarkets that require individuals to bag their own groceries. They'll still help you find the products and check you out of the store, but in exchange for reduced grocery prices you'll be bagging your items yourself when you're done.

We can also draw another analogy, a slightly more technical one. The use of radio-frequency identification (RFID) devices are being tested in supermarkets, so shoppers can simply walk out of the store and the RFID tags tell the automated checkout stand what was in the cart and how much is owed. The individual pays with his or her fingerprint and check card, and they are out the door. This can be reflected in the real estate market, as professionals will be required to find new ways to bring business in and create happy clients while reducing their chances of being replaced by electronic devices. This is all explored in far more depth in the next chapter, "The Future of Real Estate and Technology."

5

THE FUTURE OF REAL ESTATE AND TECHNOLOGY

The Internet-empowered consumer, commonly referred to as the IEC, will continue dramatically shifting the real estate industry into one where professionals will need to entirely re-create their business model and structure or be left to succumb to technology.

We can explore many future scenarios with regard to how technology will shape the future of real estate. We already know it's having an impact on finding new markets, exploring them before purchasing, and managing the property remotely.

Today's real estate industry is fueled by the advancement of technology, economics, and a changing demographic. Changes in alliances and consolidations will be minimal compared with Internet-enabled transactions about to shift the entire industry. Just a few years ago, agents worked out of large bound volumes of MLS listings that were updated every couple of weeks. This was one example of the "gatekeeper" mentality that is being broken down by an unlimited supply of free information available directly to consumers through easy search tools. Even comparative analyses are available online so a seller can appropriately price his or her home before putting it on the market. Satellite photo-graphs and mapping software provide details of the area. A con-sumer who wants to see how close his or her new house is to the beach by viewing the walking path to get there is afforded that op-portunity online. Real estate professionals still can embrace the new set of technologies about to be deployed, but they must un-derstand what they are and how to work with them first.

THE ROLE AND VALUE OF REAL ESTATE AGENTS IN THE INTERNET AGE

Numerous professional service organizations, including travel, stock, mortgage brokers, and insurance organizations have been dramatically impacted by massive technological changes in their businesses. The technological boom has affected their strat-egy, pricing, revenue, and the predictions for their business in the future. The Internet has undoubtedly played the most significant role in the shifts we've seen in other industries.

Because of the complexity of the systems involved in making a real estate deal happen, real estate professionals have been pro-tected from much of the change other industries have experi-enced. In fact, real estate agents have largely embraced technology because it's helped them do their job easier and retain more clients. As we will see throughout this book, the technology you have been embracing will soon be your largest competitor, and your fiercest to date. This chapter is dedicated to exploring the future of technology in real estate to understand how the tech-nology will have a real-world impact on the marketplace. The sheer number of real estate agents and brokers will have a detri-mental impact on their future as many are inched out of the mar-ket. The competent professionals who know how to create a niche for their services or are simply really, really good at what they do stand the biggest chance of surviving the changes the Internet is about to impose on the industry. Reinventing your business is re-ally the best approach to surviving a change with such an impact.

As real estate agents, you have relied on the fact that to subscribe to an MLS, you must be licensed and/or registered in that particular area. Major organizations such as REALTOR.com have provided access to nationwide MLS systems for their clients, and this will require rethinking what a real estate professional's true benefit to the market is. Some suggest that real estate agents need to find out who their "true friends are" and band together like a pack of wolves; but this won't shelter a real estate professional from the understated changes about to occur.

TRENDS IN THE REAL ESTATE MARKET

There are two major trends to focus on: We have those that are consumer-facing and those that are back-end or real estate professional–facing. Both of these technology trends will impact you as real estate professionals, so they both need to be considered. Consumer-facing technologies are those that will streamline or change the process of acquiring, managing, and selling real estate from an investor or primary homeowner standpoint. Back-end or real estate–facing technologies are those that will streamline processes on the real estate professionals' side of things, such as sending data to partners or creating electronic relationships.

CONSUMER-FACING TRENDS

Intelligent search engines enable consumers to find information without putting up with all the bad information that appeared when the technology first was deployed. We are beginning to see the ability to sign electronically, including the national recognition and acceptance of digital signatures and the elimination of traditional notary services in many areas and electronic-friendly companies. Sites are popping weekly that allow for price comparatives and market analyses, as well as for mortgage-rate comparisons. Watch for these tools because they will create a smarter clientele who will expect a different level and perhaps even a different type of service from you.

Access to complete transactions fully online, with integrated search, purchasing, and loan-processing information, will forever change the way individuals and/or businesses buy and complete real estate transactions.

The easier it becomes to find and apply for a mortgage online while providing required documents electronically through Web-based upload systems that streamline the entire mortgage process, the more we'll expect everything to run this smoothly.

Blogs, or Weblogs, that contain opinions on agents, real estate companies, and mortgage lenders and brokers are popping up everywhere. This also applies to property management companies. These are essentially online opinion sites. Review them; you might even find yourself on a list somewhere. Take the information and critique, positive or negative, seriously because your clients are. You might even consider "Googling" yourself or your business to see what pops up.

The ability to compare market rates online and to have multiple lenders competing for a loan is a trend we're seeing in many sectors; Lendingtree.com was a leader in the industry and others are following with even more creative systems. These types of tools will eliminate the advantage the mortgage broker has provided in the past, which is access to multiple banks and the ability to compare rates easily.

Clients have the capability to access the MLS online, providing nationwide searches on such sites as REALTOR.com, an essential component to the real estate investment crowd. Watch for new feature-rich sites and companies that no longer give the lead over to an agent, but keep it for their own salaried staff to follow up on.

Also watch for extensive for-sale-by-owner sites that allow the average consumer to list property and to have complete access to the systems agents use daily to find properties. Pay close attention to the features that these companies are offering and the advantages you once had that they are taking away. These will be important factors in the future. These systems also feed into the nationwide MLS services that are searchable by anyone with Internet access. MLS access usually includes the ability to list a lockbox code online (lockboxes are available at your local hardware store) and to share this with licensed agents. Stop ignoring those for-sale-by-owner sellers. Many times they've been advised to offer a commission and they often do.

So what do all these tools, enhancements, and Web-enabled products mean today for the consumer? They mean streamlined transactions, an incredible amount of data, and the ability to sift through it quickly based on search criteria. What about the future? Consumers can expect to completely and seamlessly complete transactions online from the loan application and sales contract to the closing of escrow and signing documents without ever having to see someone face-to-face or even talk with them by phone. You can see now why reinventing your business is so crucial.

Sites such as ehow.com tell consumers how to buy houses online. Review *www.ehow.com/how_703_shop-house-online.html* for more information. Many other sites advise clients on various aspects of transactions, and Google receives a lot of hits on various aspects of real estate deals.

TECHNOLOGY ENHANCEMENTS TO CONSIDER

Numerous technology enhancements must be considered today. Some will help your clients; others will help you more effectively manage your business. These are not designed to replace the list of recommendations noted in other chapters, but to supplement it based on where technology is headed.

Contact Management. Consider enhancing your contact management software. While traditional contact management software simply provided a list of contacts and data about individuals or businesses, some enhanced contact management software packages include the ability to manage sales funnels and send automated marketing messages to clients or potential clients and the ability to view from a "dashboard" perspective what the business is doing. Use systems that automatically notify you when certain types of homes hit various sites, including those in for-sale-by-owner sites. They just might be good matches for your buyers. You might even look for an inexpensive solution such as Goldmine or other competitors to manage sales funnels.

PDF Autogeneration. The "old" technology allows organizations to save documents in PDF format that can then be sent to clients or others involved in the transaction. However, PDF autogeneration software creates spec sheets on the fly, so consumers finding properties they are interested in can download a sheet with most of the information needed to make purchasing decisions. Some MLS companies require that you don't modify any of their data so be sure to follow their rules.

Online Forums. Perhaps one of the fastest ways to reinvent yourself as an expert in a particular area is to create a chat forum (managed by you) online. Often these forums are free and any moderately decent Web developer could have it up and running and linked to your site in an hour. Try creating forums for investors or homebuyers and organize them into folders by area or by question type. Log in regularly and answer questions, making yourself invaluable and clearly stating your expertise. Ask others to create links to your site; you can also use the data to obtain and retain new clients.

Consider Convergence. If you are running a real estate company with multiple offices, consider the possibilities that convergence, commonly referred to as VoIP, offers. Many technologies accompany most of these business-quality products. (Stay away from many of the freebies because of the quality of service, and the lack of extras will make your life much easier.) If you have an office in Los Angeles and an office in New York City, chances are your LA office frequently calls New York, all at a long-distance rate. VoIP eliminates this; it also provides least-cost routing of calls so a call from one area to the other, even if it isn't at the office, will be routed first to the office where the call will cost the least to make. This is a cost savings feature for certain types of businesses.

Unified Messaging. Adding features such as unified messaging (UM) will ensure all your voice mail ends up in your e-mail, a rather convenient feature. You can add follow-me forwarding that will forward calls to a variety of devices all preset by you, the user of the system. Management costs are also reduced because it doesn't take a rocket scientist to make changes to the phone system; a simple Windows interface and you can manage extensions, phone names, etc. Phones from some vendors are Web enabled, and some can even be configured to provide video so you and your clients or your business partners can see one another face-to-face. This is especially helpful if your primary business is to work with investors who may live or work all over the nation.

Portfolio Management Software. Virtual portfolio management software lets investors and residential owners manage their real estate portfolio online. This could be a tremendous competitive advantage! If you're one of the first, especially in your area, to provide intranet-based tools to your clients, imagine the competitive advantage. The software (you can buy off-the-shelf packages or have a Web developer create one for you) will ideally let them upload and manage photos, descriptions of the property, cash flows, investment value or equity positions, and retrieve comps directly from a site. You can provide this great, fairly inexpensive tool to your investing clients to help them get a handle on their investments.

Additionally, visually seeing their portfolio grow is often a motivating tool to encourage them to build on their portfolio. Logging in and seeing $60,000 of uninvested equity might be the kick in the pants some investors need to buy more—and give you more business. It also increases the "switching costs" of going from one agent to another who may be offering lower rates. Anything you can do to increase switching costs is a good thing in this market. It may be your expertise, or it may be the invaluable tools you provide your clients. If you're interested in this option, several commercial packages are available, or a Web developer could make a custom application that is designed to best fit your business.

E-Systems. As the Internet creates a market that is almost entirely Web based and provides incredible transaction-processing services, several technologies will be required to successfully integrate the technology into your own business. Among these are digital signature software, online notary services, wire transfer services, online contracts, and the Web enablement of many services provided by mail or fax today, including loan applications and verifications of income or employment. Pay particular attention to standards being introduced and note that they will change regularly; IT standards always do—just ask anyone in the health profession. Partner with a technology company specializing in real estate to be sure you're ready for these advanced changes that can challenge even the most savvy Web-applications expert. Also be sure that new organizations you choose to work with are Internet-friendly and Internet-savvy, which will help enable you to push your business to embrace technology as much as possible.

As a real estate professional, watch for large organizations investing a lot of money into Web-based or Web-enabled systems and look to see where they lead. This may be the first clue regarding what technology to expect in the coming year. For example, Microsoft, the largest computer software company in the world, has allied with RE/MAX International Inc., Prudential Real Estate Affiliates, and Better Homes and Gardens Real Estate Service to begin its move toward domination of the industry.

REFERRAL OR LEAD-BASED MODELS

Companies such as AgentConnect.com and RealtyNow.com have begun marketing the names of consumers who have expressed interest in a home sale or purchase, essentially generating valuable warm leads for agents. This trend appears to be on an upward move. As Web-based transactions take hold in the future, the market of lead generation probably will become more of a click-through fee than a referral fee. You should begin partnering with bigger organizations that generate leads online, even if you are a smaller player in your market—particularly if you begin to see investors take a hold in your markets—because this means that demand will be driven and supply will lessen; we've seen this time and time again over the past five years.

VIRTUAL TEAMS

Virtual teams have their place in the real estate industry, especially in franchises or in organizations that are spread throughout the nation. Consider an organization that works with investors to create portfolios and increase their equity positions. Often these organizations have agents throughout the country in their hot markets, and they may provide property-management services and other offerings to make life easier for the investor. This rather new trend of one-stop shopping in real estate investing has been quite the moneymaker for many businesses. These types of organizations, which are positioned to be quite successful in the future given the right technology, are ripe for the creation of virtual teams, and technology leads the way in their success.

Some agents specialize in only representing buyers or sellers as a way to compete in a constantly changing market. Often buyers search the Internet to find properties prior to contacting agents, and then contact agents once they've identified areas or properties for purchase. Agents can create virtual teams of individuals to assist them in the process of finding, acquiring, and closing deals in areas their investors may wish to purchase in. Technology has helped lead the way in virtual teaming and has provided a means by which organizations can successfully manage a remote company. Because these buyers and sellers usually find the agents or properties online, they are great resources for testing many of the virtual team models that include using technology to hold virtual meetings, signing paperwork "virtually," and creating a virtual office that may have "local offices" in a variety of locations simply through partnership arrangements.

In virtual teams, we often see marketing assistants, agents in other areas, lender representatives, and transaction coordinators accessed and communicated with through virtual means primarily if not exclusively. Tools such as NetMeeting and Skype can provide great communication methods with little cost but great benefit. Many of the individuals these organizations or professionals work with are working out of home offices or their workplaces can be anywhere with high-speed Internet connections. Virtual private networks (VPNs) allow for secure communications across the Internet and are relatively inexpensive and simple to install. VPNs have increased efficiency and security far beyond expectations and are critical when creating a virtual team. Virtual teams offer you or your organization the tremendous expertise (the best of the best) with reasonable cost and very low overhead. Virtual teams by nature do not have an office; they may meet for lunch or while on business travel. Alternative methods of communication include videoconferencing and instant messaging, as well as shared calendars over the VPN and an intranet portal that provides each member of the organization with current information on the company.

PAPERLESS TRANSACTIONS

Currently, the average number of checkpoints a single transaction has to go through is 128. While this is an average and may be higher or lower, it does help to explain the incredible complication of real estate transactions and all the checks and balances that enter into the transaction. This complication has been one of the great barriers in the Internet transformation of the real estate industry. One example of a paperless transaction system is from SureClose, available online at *www.sureclose.com/*. SureClose is a product of Stewart Realty Solutions (SRS), one of the leaders in paperless transaction management systems for real estate, closing, and mortgage industries, according to its Web site. It provides digital transformation and management of real estate files for every listing, sale, closing, and/or loan file.

Because many processes are involved in a real estate transaction, they create a situation difficult for technology staff to mimic using computers. Many of these processes are a result of legal obligations or liability reduction. Complicated standards, a lot of intraorganization communication, and difficulty in creating a seamless system to mimic this process has slowed the technological progression in the real estate industry. Most agree that in the next two years these hurdles will be overcome and paperless transactions will go enter the mainstream.

For the past few years, two major industry efforts have attempted to work through the issues of technology standards in this industry—the Real Estate Transaction Standard (RETS) group and the Mortgage Industry Standards Maintenance Organization (MISMO). Since 1999 when it was founded by the Mortgage Bankers Association (MBA), MISMO has led the way for technology to transform the lending process from one too cumbersome with many paper processes to an electronic one. Its Web site at *www.mismo.com* provides the latest versions of standards right on its home page. It also includes eMortgage guidelines and recommendations built on the XML data specs. If you are a mortgage broker or lender, pay very close attention to this! Adopting these standards may lower costs by as much as $249 per loan, according to a study commissioned by the MBA the past year.

Attendees at a convention in Orlando, Florida, in October 2005 received their first glimpse at e-mortgages and a guide in offering them to their customer base. While this is an executive-level guide to e-mortgage implementations, return on investment, legal issues, and industry processes, this is the beginning of a revolutionary change we will begin to see in late 2006. The need for multiple partners in the e-mortgage processes stagnated the growth of this technology for some time, but most major companies are now on board and committing both research and development and IT dollars to these efforts.

The Securable, Manageable, Achievable, Retrievable, and Transferable guide (referred to as SMART) was released by MISMO as a primary tool for using electronic mortgages. SMART Docs capture, store, and record data in an electronic format that reduces the manual process in loan origination and closing.

In addition to the upcoming e-mortgage guide, another major milestone for MISMO has been the publication of a SMART Doc specification guide. SMART docs are the MISMO version of a document formatted in XML and are considered the key to unlocking savings in electronic mortgages.

"Sometimes people mistakenly say, 'Well, it's just paper, so let's just convert the paper to electronic,'" the *Register* said. "But you learn very quickly that is not the case." And that's why the SMART Doc specifications were created. Five lenders in the country generate about 60 percent of all real estate business according to the same source, so once these lenders adopt the e-mortgage process, the rest of the companies will have to convert quickly just to keep up.

MISMO partnered in 2005 with the Appraisal Institute to develop data standards to complete the valuation and mortgage lending bridge. It is also working with organizations representing notaries and county recorder offices. Electronic notes are also beginning to emerge, helping to increase the usability of the technology. These electronic notes, or e-notes, will represent the collateral on the loan, particularly when it is sold in the secondary market. It will also work for consumers who won't receive a paper note anymore. Even secondary mortgage organization Fannie Mae accepts electronic notes, and Freddie Mac is working on accepting e-notes soon. Many organizations are focusing now on how to make these systems as secure as possible, reduce the potential for fraud, and maintain client confidentiality while still creating a system that will track progress. In 2006, the RETS community is expected to develop the RETS 2 specifications to standardize security issues. These systems will bridge the gap to a complete paperless transaction and push the industry toward this level of integration.

According to the RETS Web site, "The Real Estate Transaction Standard (RETS) is the open standard for exchanging real estate transaction information. Consisting of a transaction specification and a standard Extensible Markup Language (XML) Document Type Definition (DTD), RETS is being implemented by many real estate industry leaders in their next generation of real estate information systems." We've found this is the case when conducting secondary research, which is another important technology to pay close attention to if you are in the real estate business.

PARTNERSHIPS AND POWERFUL ENTITIES

Microsoft has entered, with great concern from NAR, into the Web-based business. RealSelect Inc. (a subsidiary of Homestore Inc., and the operator of REALTOR.com), and the association have begun asking MLS organizations for exclusive rights to listings in exchange for cash under a "Gold Alliance" program. All MLS organizations that provide listing data to competing Web sites would be required to terminate the relationship within a year and a half. Any MLS organizations that decline to sign up for the program can still provide listings to REALTOR.com, but they won't be paid for their listings. Watching Microsoft's move with these organizations is a sign of the domination of Web-based systems in the future of real estate. Alliances like this that eliminate entire market segments may prove to damage you more than help you, and eventually may not even be considered legal. For example, in

1998 Intuit and RealSelect entered into a strategic alliance for financial services that became a very powerful entity.

You should be aware of the affiliation with the following organizations because of their incredible power in the markets: Homestore Inc. is a media and technology solutions company that helps both the real estate professionals and the consumers. The Homestore Network is the largest of all the real estate agent sites on the Internet. It includes REALTOR.com, which is the official site of the National Association of REALTORS®. It also includes HomeBuilder.com, which is the official site of the National Association of Home Builders. Included in the portfolio is RENTNET, an apartment, corporate housing, and self-storage resource. SeniorHousingNet, a resource for senior housing and care, is also a prominent site on the Internet. Homestore.com, owned by the same organization, is a site for home-related information with a mortgage-financing emphasis. These sites attract more than 9 million individuals per month, according to the NAR.

The work doesn't end here. Homestore has a professional software division that provides real estate professionals with CRM and inventory tools. TOP PRODUCER is the number one contact management software for real estate agents, according to the NAR. The Enterprise edition offers real estate professionals custom Web and video production services and may be software worth considering. They have incredible investment numbers for the previous years and are working with organizations such as Habitat for Humanity to help feed their marketing and reach out to the community.

The reach of these organizations is widespread. Content from Homestore feeds the Home & Real Estate Channel for America Online, which we have already discussed with regard to power in the industry. It also feeds the House and Home Channel for MSN. Welcome Wagon is another service that has been introducing community businesses to new homeowners and renters for decades, and Homestore Plans & Publications sells branded magazines with home plans and construction-ready floor plans to consumers and homebuilders. You can see from this incredible business how powerful and large-reaching NAR is with regard to technology. Homestore is a publicly traded organization under the ticker HOMS.

Microsoft and Intuit have partnered to offer an online opportunity to shop for loans. The Massachusetts Institute of Technology has a Center for Real Estate designed to improve the technology environment and help inform real estate professionals. RealBird Inc., a provider of online map-based Internet Data Exchange (IDX) property search Web sites and GIS tools for real estate, partnered with MLSsoftware.com to resell a branded version of RealBird's service to its clients. According to the *National Real Estate Investor,* Constellation Real Technology Partners, a consortium of 14 real estate companies and investment firms, invested $30.5 million in four technology companies with the goal of investing in companies developing technology such as Web-based property tax software, contract, project management, or e-procurement services.

APPLICATIONS AND CASE STUDIES

As mentioned earlier, several software companies are interested in the real estate business, a fascinating but not surprising move. Real estate agents don't only compete with one another; they compete now with low-cost or flat-fee online brokers and soon with more powerful software than ever. The Microsoft case studies list refers to numerous organizations that have been assisted by Microsoft to increase productivity and efficiency. Read through each of these case studies that may pertain to you for ideas on how to integrate technology into your business: *members. microsoft.com/CustomerEvidence/Search/AdvancedSearchResults. aspx?Flag=0&AndTaxID=25185&AndTaxID=3282.* Even the MLS has jumped on board with expansion and tools from Microsoft. Case studies include small real estate organizations, individual private professionals, all the way to large organizations in a variety of ancillary market segments.

An organization called a la mode inc. offers solutions to real estate professionals that include appraisers, mortgage companies, inspectors, etc. Their XSites Network ties real estate professionals together with advanced transaction management tools. You can research their products further at *www.alamode.com/Default.aspx.* Keep in mind this is a tool that will allow you to communicate with most of those involved in the real estate transaction; this may be one way for you to compete with online organizations that provide cradle-to-grave services for consumers.

THE ONGOING BATTLE: LEGAL TROUBLE

Many agents using traditional models are attempting to undermine the efforts made by online discount brokers and Web-based systems. A turf war has begun recently in the industry, and it's beginning to make a profound mark on real estate. Internet companies are becoming more popular than ever, and the battle lines have been drawn. On one side are more traditional real estate companies, brokers, and agents who have teamed up with the state commissions that regulate them. These organizations firmly believe that the real estate world is complicated, and that buyers and sellers need hand-holders through the entire process or risk suffering from their decisions.

On the other side of the battle are Internet companies and Washington—yes, the government. In March 2005, the Justice Department filed a complaint against the Kentucky Real Estate Commission, stating that rules prohibiting brokers from giving consumers rebates on real estate commissions violated antitrust laws. Ten other states have similar rules, and some experts expect other suits to follow. Doing so may give a large boost to the Internet camp. The rebate strategy is a key for some brokers such as ZipRealty, who market online and give a portion of their commissions back to the sellers at the close of escrow. RealEstate.com gives consumers gift cards instead of money, a practice also in-cluded in the suit.

Agents argue that letting online brokers sell a basic version of their service without performing certain duties like negotiating prices wouldn't be fair to consumers. Some experts believe the unbundling of services is one of the survival techniques that agents can use to fight the "Internet chaos." Austin lobbyist Bill Miller, representing the Texas Association of REALTORS, has noted in newspapers that rules such as requiring a minimum level of service are there to protect consumers, leaving the agent un-able to unbundle services.

In the world of real estate, one of the most common ways to create your own business is to buy a franchise from a big company like Cendant Corporation, which runs Century 21 and Coldwell Banker, or RE/MAX International. These agencies charge com-missions of 5 percent to 6 percent of the purchase price to the seller for their services.

DISCOUNT BROKERAGE COMPANIES

Online discounters such as the New York area Foxtons North America may charge as little as 3 percent. ZipRealty charges 5 per-cent to 6 percent but gives 25 percent of the commission back to the sellers after the close of escrow. Even though some of the dis-counters expect the seller to take a more active role, such as hold-ing open houses or negotiating prices, some are reaching substantial market share even in urban areas. ZipRealty, which went public in 2004, may earn $10 million on more than $100 mil-lion in revenue in 2005, even though it doesn't even have 1 per-cent of the market share in any market where it conducts business. The costs of doing business are quite low while its ser-vice levels don't seem to bother many sellers. ZipRealty has noted that its agents sell about twice as many homes as their competi-tors do. It has very few offices and finds clients by online advertising or telemarketing rather than employing agents throughout the country.

In December 2005, *Los Angeles Times* writer Annette Haddad wrote about the low-priced brokerage companies that were making their marks on real estate in an article titled, "Low-priced brokerage is shaking up real estate." Some of these discounted brokers, such as CataList, were noted in the article as openly mocking traditional brokers, its competitors. CataList is working hard in California to change the way homes are sold, charging homesellers half of what commission-based brokers do at 3 percent of the sales price without infringing on service. Agents of the organization will be paid as full-time salaried employees rather than as independent contractors, while using the Web site as a portal for local housing price data. The founder of the organization, who cofounded Grubb & Ellis, a Bay Area commercial property management firm that grew into one of the largest publicly traded commercial real estate companies, noted: "We knew that this kind of business model would be highly disruptive and evoke a response." The Hermosa Beach–based organization provides full service at significantly reduced commissions, forcing down the cost of residential real estate transactions just as it did with online stock trading and travel. The founder believes, contrary to some industry experts, that as home values slow and values stop rising as fast, homesellers will think hard before giving 6 percent of their sales price to a real estate agent.

In the example noted previously, the organization is spending about twice the average for marketing—about $2,500 per customer—to attract and promote listings through brochures and expensive radio and newspaper ads. Still, it is a growing organization that is expanding into the northern California markets. Agents earned $60 billion in fees the past year on the standard commission rate, raising eyebrows of consumer advocates and even the Justice Department. One barrier to this model is how the buyers' agents are paid, which is commission based. Many of the discount brokers offer only 1.5 percent, half of the usual 3 percent, and they are having a hard time attracting agents to bring them buyers. Organizations using this model will have to network and change their image of being the bad guy in the pricing wars.

Real estate professionals can win the war with the Internet. By reshaping their business model and finding new strategies, they can successfully compete with low-cost and flat-fee online brokers and with new technology that will streamline the processes they once carried out or facilitated manually. Embrace the change, find your new niche, and do it today before it's too late!

6

SO WHAT CAN YOU DO ABOUT IT?

If you are a real estate profes-
sional, you're asking the obvious question: "If she's right, what
am I going to do about it?" There's a lot you can do about it! This
is not a hopeless situation, but it will require you to stop and rethink your business plan and reengineer the way you work with
clients.

Figuring out solutions to entire shifts in an industry is not
easy. The suggestions I am outlining in this book are based on several key factors: research, analysis of other industries, experience
in IT and its history as well as its future (as much as one can predict that), understanding of generational differences, and experience in the real estate industry. Each is a possibility, of course, not
a surefire way to approach this problem. One thing is evident,
however; without action, the real estate professionals who try to
do business the same way they've been doing business won't suc-
ceed in the new Internet market. Certainly, looking at environmental issues and those who have been both successful and
unsuccessful can shed some light on this topic. I'm going to be
very blunt in this chapter because you need accurate information

that will help you survive the changing industry. Not every solution will be a good one for each reader, but something is bound to click and you will need to brainstorm possible new ways of doing business.

THE CONTROL OF RESOURCES

Real estate agents and mortgage brokers have employed a number of processes and controls to maintain their positions, as we've already discovered. You have dominated the market by controlling resources, including information about what buyers are looking and what homes are for sale. Sellers not working with buyers' agents wouldn't have access to the buyers who would pay them a commission. We have discussed most of this in the information about real estate agents in particular, and how they have protected their trade.

Access to the MLS, historically, was well constrained. Generally speaking, the only efficient way to sell a home was through the MLS listing. If only agents have access to the MLS, then only agents have control over the market. Many brokers and agencies lobbied against "for sale" signs on properties, again restricting the ability of a homeowner to sell his or her property directly. These rules still exist in some areas, especially in association-controlled areas.

Agents have also controlled walk-through visits by way of the lockbox. This handy device allows those who have a special code into the home of a seller because the box contains a key to the house. It is very convenient for sellers to allow agents to show their property when they are not home, while setting the ground rules for entry, such as a phone call two hours prior to visiting or restricting hours. Sellers and buyers can work directly to arrange showings, but buyers sometimes find this inconvenient, and sellers who work during the day may be restricted to evening or nighttime showings and open houses strictly on weekends. With many for-sale-by-owner sites now, an individual can list his or her lockbox number that is accessible only by licensed agents or brokers, giving the security and convenience of an agent's offering without paying the commissions associated with it. This is the same mechanism by which you, the professional, have secured lockboxes, only now your clients can do it themselves.

Agents were also legitimized because of the restrictions placed on buyers and sellers. Some of the contracts used could be quite complicated to the individual who sells a home only every few years. This lack of knowledge and know-how legitimized agents in real estate much the same as complicated mortgage paperwork, competing and changing interest rates, and loan programs legitimized brokers who acted as intermediaries of information.

TECHNOLOGICAL RESEARCH

Let's start with the first of these factors—research. Research shows that technological shifts create dramatic change in almost any industry known to man. No industry, absolutely none, has remained unchanged alongside concurrent changes in technology. While some change more than others, a cursory review of technology literature and its history outlines the dramatic impacts, whether over a short or long period of time. It's really all relative: The Internet has created change at a far more rapid pace than we've seen in the past. In many ways, this is the second revolution of industry and this one is also, in many ways, more powerful. We have truly globalized our economy and created a true international marketplace. The Internet will continue to do this, but stated laws in IT theory indicate that once technology begins transforming, the pace only increases with slight road bumps along the way. The complexity of real estate transaction was a road bump—note the word *was*.

IT think tanks and cutting-edge organizations are creating a way to sort through vast amounts of data at an astounding rate, all while making it extremely accessible to anyone with an Internet connection, broadband preferably, of course. Key organizations are spending great amounts of money to learn to sort, organize, and share information quickly and efficiently, and many companies are spending a lot of money to happily take away your clients and your money.

Couple this with the ability to complete online transactions, move money from one place to another, digitally sign documents, and search for property that meets investment or residence criteria easily and quickly, and you have a market-transforming paradigm shift. This paradigm shift is what will require real estate professionals to change the way they do business, but there are options in this new marketplace.

TRADITIONAL REAL ESTATE PROCESS

Traditionally, real estate agents have matched buyers and sellers. The agents give the buyers and sellers advice and information to help start and follow through on the transaction. An agent (known as the listing agent) lists the property and determines the asking price, guides the seller to give the property curb appeal and charm, advertises the property, including listing it on the MLS, and works with buyers or buyers' agents in the screening process and showing the home. When offers are received, the seller's agent helps negotiate the transaction and, in return, the seller pays a commission to the listing agent. This commission must be paid regardless of how the buyer is found.

The buyer's agent, working on a portion of the commission from the seller's agent, helps find properties for the buyer. The buyer will walk through many homes arranged by his or her agent, make a decision, and then the buyer's agent works through paperwork with the seller's agent.

Depending on the market, different aspects of this process will be more important. For example, if real estate is in high demand (a seller's market), an agent can provide a great service to buyers by passing on information about newly offered properties and may, in fact, demand a premium for this information. Conversely, in a buyer's market, an agent can be of great help in marketing a property and locating buyers.

Once offers are made, contingencies on the contract must be met. Often, contingencies include the buyer's ability to get financing and the seller's ability to have the home pass its inspection. Usually, banks require appraisals to meet at least the purchase price of the property, so appraisal contingencies are common. Agents often refer buyers and sellers to appraisers, home warranty companies, lenders, etc.

There are also numerous contracts between the buyers and the sellers, and the agents and the other agencies. Most real estate agents work for a brokerage company, which may employ many real estate agents. In addition to the contracts among agents and buyers and sellers, the relationships between agents and agencies are contractual.

Agents with access to the MLS possess several proprietary pieces of information. They have access to the lockbox combinations for convenient access to show a property. They have information about previous owners and how many outstanding liens against the property exist. They also have access to information about the land, when the home was built, and public records such as property tax data.

In the traditional model, others play a role; as discussed, these organizations include title agencies, insurance agencies, lenders, brokers, escrow companies, appraisers, etc.

WEB-BASED SCENARIO

Imagine the following scenario: Your potential client researches using his or her favorite search engine in what other investors believe is the next hottest market. He or she then verifies the information with bloggers on a Web site geared toward real estate investors and looks up demographic information on numerous other Web sites to check average income, unemployment rates, and appreciation in this area.

The consumer then determines that this particular area is a good market to be in and proceeds to search for two properties (one single-family residence and one duplex) in the market. He or she identifies two properties using a search tool that not only shows the property, but instantly reveals monthly and yearly cash flow, rental comparatives (rental comps, or what the property can rent for), cash on cash and other return on investment figures, taxes, a quote for insurance with a link to the least expensive provider, and utility payments with links to the utilities for turn-on. After clicking on the pictures and viewing the history of the home including title, the individual determines that they are both good investments and hits the "add to cart" button. Essentially, the buyer is purchasing two homes entirely online.

The next step in this process includes making an official offer to the seller, or using a "buy-it-now" feature, mimicking an option eBay introduced to buy an item that is usually negotiable (or auctioned) for a fixed price under certain conditions, which allows the buyer and seller to agree on the seller's terms up front with a guaranteed closing. Let's assume the seller for the single-family home has a buy-it-now option that the buyer agrees to, while the seller for the duplex wants to negotiate terms. The Web site that the buyer is using allows him or her to choose the options he or she wants in the contract, such as "loan contingency" or "five-day inspection period." After all this is done, the "document" is electronically signed online and then submitted to the seller who receives an e-mail to view the offer. He or she makes updates or a counteroffer online or rejects it altogether, and this process continues until either one party backs out of the negotiations or an acceptable agreement is reached.

Once contracts are signed by both parties online, the escrow company receives an electronic copy and secures a title agency electronically. The digital signature is verified, and the seller receives an e-mail with multiple offers from banks that have already seen his or her credit report, know the cost and value of the property, the down payment inputted into the initial system, and the status of the residence. The seller chooses a bank by looking at a matrix of each of the major points on the loan (prepayment penalties, interest rates, and total closing costs), one is selected online, and within three days the buyer has the mortgage company's blessing to close the deal. The mortgage company has been linked to the escrow company on the "back end" of the system, and information has been securely passed from one company to another during the entire process.

Near completion of the transaction, the bids for insurance come in. The buyer selects an insurance company online and is asked if he or she wants property management on the home. The buyer knows that the single-family residence will not be rented out, but the duplex will be. There is currently one unit vacant and it needs to be rented. The buyer selects a property manager, again based on a matrix of criteria such as percentage cost, the length and terms of the contract, and the average days to rent in the area. Prior to submitting the contract, the buyer looks at an online opinion site of those who have used the service company and finds it to be acceptable. An electronic contract is sent to the property management company and the day escrow closes, the property manager begins advertising for the property and setting up direct deposit for rental income checks. The buyer is given contact information for the property manager, and a daily status update is sent out automatically on the effort to rent out the unit.

The buyer electronically wires funds to escrow and the seller then gets to "rate" the buyer, much the same that eBay allows and encourages its buyers and sellers to rate one another on service and product to encourage a safe trading environment. After exchanging positive feedbacks, the buyer and seller have completed their deal, all within days of starting it.

Now, rethink your marketing campaign. In this type of scenario, which *will* be the case within a few years, how will you compete? Where do you see yourself adding value and fitting into this type of model? Where is the need for the real estate professional (which niche is your choice), and how will you find your role in this scenario? The technology to do all of this is available today and is being developed for implementation in the real estate industry. IT professionals are working day and night to make this a reality, and it will occur sooner rather than later. Your marketing campaign and how you actually do business will have to overcome the power of this type of tool and service, and the time to figure out what it will be is now.

NEW MARKETING—FIRST AND FOREMOST

Everyone has suggestions; mine are based on talking with clients, my knowledge and expertise in IT management, and my experience and credentials in strategizing a business around technology. Initially, your marketing campaign (regardless of what professional industry you are in pertaining to real estate) will need to be modified. Maintaining the same marketing campaign while competing in an entirely different market will not improve the position of your business. One suggestion is to stop using scare tactics. The consumer who will be happy trading property in this secure online environment will not succumb to scare tactics used today about how complicated and scary the process of buying and selling real estate is. It isn't scary and it isn't complicated. Putting the right people in place on your team (such as a real estate attorney and an escrow company) means that the agent, for instance, isn't necessarily needed, and considerable money is saved if a consumer is the one selling the property without using an agent. People who are comfortable making these electronic wire transfers and completing entire transactions online aren't going to be scared off by the tactics used by many professional real estate organizations today. A new marketing campaign must be developed to retain existing clients and attract new ones immediately after you determine what your niche will be.

ANALYSIS OF OTHER INDUSTRIES

Focusing on other industries that have experienced remarkable changes in the way their businesses have been handled over the past five years shows us incredible amounts of data that, in some regard, are almost frightening for many industries. The Internet has shifted entire markets, eliminated many businesses, created conglomerates and companies that are run by IT professionals, initiated and supported a global marketplace, created an online identity for nearly every individual in our nation, and created businesses at the same time—all while drastically changing those left behind. Try to think of a business today not affected—greatly—by the Internet. You will be hard-pressed to do so.

Even those who act as suppliers for manufacturing companies or trucking companies, which traditionally didn't move rapidly with technological change, have been drastically modified. Suppliers are required to fulfill on-demand or just-in-time reordering from their customers. They have created electronic fulfillment systems; they can track where every order is in a warehouse; and they know at any given moment, through executive dashboards, exactly where the business stands, what the issues are, and what business is at risk. They can even predict with software at any moment what their profit-and-loss numbers will be for that month, quarter, or year based on what's happening that day and what the trends have been over a given period of time. These organizations are warehousing data, turning it into information, and mining the heck out of it to truly learn about their customers, their suppliers, their supply chain, and their business.

Even more traditional industries, such as the trucking industry, for example, that are quite brick and mortar are changing significantly. Trucking industries have adopted global positioning systems (GPSs) to track the whereabouts of any of their assets (trucks or individuals) at any given time. Data fed into the system estimate arrival dates, and shipping companies will take such information and feed it into their systems. These systems then provide up-to-the-minute tracking of packages, which is then fed into electronic stores for customers to access the same data tied to their order. The process and the amount of data generated to and from these systems are overwhelming to even think about. There is not one system in operation today in any major organization that does not tie in somehow to the system in another organization, whether live or in "batch" mode (uploading or downloading data or feeds on a scheduled basis). If a traditional business like the trucking business has been so drastically modified by technology, why would a real estate professional think the same won't happen to his or her profession? Yet, looking at the data in our chapter on research, we see that there is a naive approach to what is about to happen.

WHAT ABOUT SERVICE COMPANIES?

A common argument to the newly derived theory of IT turning services into commodities is that services are human-being oriented and are therefore difficult to emulate with an online system. That is true in areas where having human contact is of value, for example, at the doctor's office (though a case can be made for that, too). Let's take a look at service industries, those even closer tied with real estate. Real estate is (or was), after all, a people business. Face-to-face interactions meant something, and although they still do in some instances, that is less the case today. Face-to-face has less value nowadays than it did a decade ago, and what is becoming increasingly important are rapid transactions, integrated systems, and efficiency. We see this with ATM use, booking travel, trading stocks—you name it.

We've looked at the travel industry before, but let's look at it again. Travel agents were valued for their knowledge of places to go, the comfort they provided by having a point of contact, their expertise in booking travel, and their access to information that most people didn't have. Slowly, technological evolution took away these advantages. Before a trip to China and with the click of a mouse and the use of a search engine, I could learn anything

I wanted to know about where to eat (or not eat) and shop in Shanghai. A consumer can easily find out the opinions of others, using sites like Epinions.com. Even travel sites let consumers rate their experiences at various places like hotels. Anyone with an ax to grind or a story to tell could easily post it online for others to see. In a sense, we have more information than we could possibly want or do anything with. Perhaps the biggest problem of all is being able to sort through that information, and great companies with gigantic goals such as Google are working on that problem. No longer did the travel agent have the benefit of knowledge and opinions that the consumer didn't. In fact, generally speaking, if we agree that the opinions of many are more valuable than the biased opinion of one, it's more valuable to get opinions online than from so-called travel experts. These experts' views were often tainted by where their biggest kickbacks, usually in the form of free trips, came from. In a sense, we were comforted by a biased opinion, a few credentials, and a complicated-looking old-style computer interface sitting on the individual's desk.

Travel experts offered the benefit of a single point of contact, and someone to phone in an emergency. The online sites that popped up quickly realized this was a barrier to entry and provided 24/7 hotlines with access to any reservation and the ability to solve almost any problem with a quick phone call or the click of a mouse. Most publish international numbers as well. Suddenly, this barrier to entry no longer existed, and the travel agent had one less opportunity to hold onto business.

Travel agents were involved often because of their expertise of the systems and the booking process, all of the steps involved, and they had seemingly quick access to plan an entire trip for the consumer. They booked the hotel, the rental car, and the airline, making sure transfers were in place, and setting up a ride to the hotel from the airport—all packaged in a neat little travel booklet with vouchers and coupons. Suddenly, the market is blessed with online travel sites such as Expedia.com or Travelocity.com, which revolutionize the world of travel. They offer online vacations, in fact booking the entire trip with a few mouse clicks, and a lot of information available to consumers to compare and contrast options and view others opinions, all while making informed decisions. Yet again, another competitive advantage the in-person agent has is whisked away by technology. In fact, the consumer gets better information, faster, and can compare rates effectively, thus saving money. The bias that was inherent in the information provided by the agent was no longer a factor in the decision-making process.

The last straw for the travel professional was the transparency of information. No longer did one individual or profession have access to the perfect information. The playing field was leveled, and, in addition to information, the companies offering online competition actually put their money where their data were and offered a way to actually complete an entire transaction using a credit card. They offered the ability to phone and experience the touchy-feely service many consumers were used to and wanted while saving money. In fact, many of the agents went to work for these organizations as experts in various areas or as call-center staff.

Many argued at the time that it would not be possible to do this because airlines required data, rental car company pricing information had to be compared, and hotels had to be rated—not to mention the deals that had to be worked between the online travel companies and the hotel and airline industries. Yet, they managed to pull it off: An array of information was compiled into one neat, searchable site that took an amazingly difficult process and made it incredibly simple for the consumer. The back-end technology may be complicated, but that's a technological issue, not a practical one. Plenty of IT folks who enjoy their jobs will be more than happy to work out any issue as it arises. These companies are pulling it off and doing it well, and every year they take more and more business from those operating in traditional models. Corporations still used travel agencies until recently; now while many still do, these travel companies are highly Webified, if not entirely so.

By now you've certainly seen the correlations between the travel industry and the real estate industry—complicated transactions with multiple parties put into one easy-to-use system. Sites include automated booking and even some negotiation (depending on the site) of price online—full support with no compromise of service, many would argue, while reduction of costs all the way around. The transitions the travel industry has seen over the past decade are beginning to happen to real estate, and it's only a matter of time before the change is just as intense. By looking at what those who have been successful through the change have done, and analyzing the steps those who were eliminated took, we can put some logic to the steps real estate professionals need to do today to prepare for tomorrow.

Other industries also are being impacted by technology, and many of them have some common themes. The rules have been revised for several industries, and the Internet is threatening to make headway in at least six more major industries in the next 24 months: jewelry, telecommunications, hotels, real estate, software, and online bill paying. The jewelry business is proving quite profitable online where precious gemstones can be purchased for 50 percent or less when compared with major retailers. Blue Nile Inc., in business for five years, made $27 million on $129 million in sales the past year. Ken Gassman of the New York newsletter organization Rapaport, noted that the upstarts "are going to kill everyone."

About 60 percent of the remaining public Internet companies made money in the fourth quarter of 2004. Venture capital investments are more than $5 billion in the first quarter of 2005 for the first time in two years. Telecommunications companies are pumping money into competing services, such as Verizon Communications' $2 billion investment in network phone technology over a two-year period. This is essentially the traditional players reinventing themselves to compete with newcomers.

Some companies, particularly in the hotel business, are threatening their chains that work with online partners. For example, InterContinental Hotels Group fines and threatens hotel owners if they partner with online organizations. Cendant Corporation is putting pressure on the NAR to make it harder for online upstarts to obtain home sales listings. However, this appears to be backfiring; hotel owners who cannot offer Web discounts are seeing travelers book elsewhere, and Cendant's inquiry has helped initiate an antitrust investigation that could leave the real estate industry in a very big quandary.

Online bill paying has been another example of technology impacting profits. Writing checks costs banks about 30 cents per check to process. Paying the same bill online costs about ten cents, thus the push for banks to encourage consumers to use available bill-pay technology. Gartner, Inc., estimated that 65 million people paid at least one bill online in 2004, up 97 percent from the prior year.

In the early days of the online revolution, most organizations targeted commodities: books, stocks, or other products. The start-up companies of today are putting together complex processes and mimicking them with online systems, allowing consumers to make smarter choices and see more alternatives. There is a large trend, especially in start-up Internet companies, to offer services with an incredible amount of uncomplicated information.

Within the six industries we see evolving in the next two years are several common threads. These companies possess a long list of middlemen, all of whom cut into profits by eating up their slices. Diamonds from South Africa may be touched by four middlemen: rough diamond brokers, cutters, jewelry wholesalers, and diamond wholesalers, for instance. Blue Nile connects over the Internet to suppliers who buy the stones directly from the De-Beers Consolidated Mines Ltd. in South Africa. It will be fascinating to watch the incredible changes under way in the economy and in the service businesses, but it's vital if you're in one of these industries or others so dangerously impacted that you are prepared for what is to come.

REVEALING IT STUDIES TO HELP YOU STRATEGIZE

You may ask why studying IT is relevant to figuring out how to navigate the drastic change about to occur in real estate. The answer is simple. By looking at the past and the way IT has changed other industries as well as the motivation of IT professionals, we can perhaps glimpse where the market may head and why. This will give real estate professionals a chance to act now before it's too late.

Technologists are motivated (and paid) to make businesses efficient. In the past, technologists were primarily a commodity; we provided a service or a backbone for the rest of the business to do their business but were often the redheaded stepchild, overlooked by business owners, CEOs, and CFOs in small and large companies. In other words, we provided the phones and the punch cards and let the business do its thing. As IT developed and began revolutionizing businesses, the focus shifted to how to make a business run better and provide greater communication and, suddenly, we came into our own. After that happened, nothing has slowed the exciting revolution that technology, particularly a consumer-friendly Internet, has brought. There are many theories on the phases of IT growth within an organization and what they do at each stage.

We installed messaging systems (known today as e-mail), we created small local area networks (LANs) to share data, and the world of IT began to change. Around that time, many books and studies were published on IT becoming a competitive advantage, and sure enough it did. In the 1990s, companies were trying to figure out ways to use IT to actually make the business run smarter, to redesign processes (hence the term *process reengineering* became mainstream), and in many cases to replace people with more efficient and cheaper technology—cheaper over the long term within the constraints of return-on-investment analysis. We saw the stock prices of these technology companies go through the roof and subsequently fall because of their lack of price substance.

Soon the computer replaced the worker, and more and more IT people were hired because they understood IT and business. Business schools created IT management programs, and many individuals graduated with a greater understanding of the impact we have, both good and bad, on business. Business alignment became a key focus, and a tremendous effort was placed on helping IT people understand the business better so they could contribute at a higher level. What many businesspeople did not expect is that a technology developed to protect against military attack would actually create an entire new marketplace and revolutionize the world.

The Internet was developed by the government in cooperation with universities when in its early form (referred to as the ARPANET), it was designed so that one node, if broken, would not cripple or disable other nodes. In other words, if a military strike took down one government system, by connecting it to others that could communicate, the system would not be crippled in its entirety. This worked tremendously well, and many of us remember the early days of the Internet that were entirely text based.

Over a period of two decades, developers created a protocol called Hypertext Transfer Protocol, or HTTP. Today we know HTTP, and we use it to reach destinations all over the Web. HTTP made the Internet, which had grown in popularity and had an increasing number of nodes, more usable and people-friendly. With the use of other systems like Domain Name Services (DNS), people were able to type in names of places like furniture.com, rather than having to remember the long string of numbers referred to as an Internet Protocol (IP) address that the server resides on. Thus, this technology did two major things. First, it truly enhanced, in epic proportions, the value IT could add to businesses. Second, the Internet created an entirely new medium that was Web based and virtual—not only a new market segment but an entire industry.

Companies like eBay didn't have brick-and-mortar stores before they had their online store. Amazon.com wasn't selling books in a retail store before going online. These companies had entirely new businesses that were started on the Internet based on an entirely new modality. Technology had, for the first time, created an entire industry—something unseen prior to that. At the same time, it was continuing to enhance companies that were primarily brick and mortar yet embracing the idea of Web enablement while the consumer began to become irritated and antsy with organizations that didn't offer online solutions or access to their traditional information through online mediums.

Existing companies quickly put up Web sites to become "Webified," but this is only Web enablement, not Web based, and Web based is where the future lies These same companies figured out how to integrate shopping carts, calculated by zip code the cost of shipping and sales tax, and learned out how to determine if a product was in stock in the warehouse (or in the supplier's warehouse)—all instantaneously. These little challenges were all incredibly complicated in the beginning. Suddenly, system integration was critical to any business' survival, and IT workers scrambled to make legacy (old) and current systems, never designed to talk with one another, communicate seamlessly.

As the Internet grew, intranets became more popular. Companies provided in-house information to their own internal customers, or employees, in a portal solution to link them to other applications within the organization. Some took these further and allowed employees to do "radical" things such as elect benefits online and file complaints anonymously with a Web form. For technologists, local area networks grew to huge wide area networks, and the virtualization began. Phone communication was replaced by instant messaging, e-mail, and Voice over IP (VoIP); everything became a part of something else; and we had a new revolution through technological integration.

At the same time, entire industries that were strictly Web based were popping up all over the place. As mentioned earlier, Amazon.com, Overstock.com, and eBay.com, to name three, became household names. While some people were still skeptical of security, the two youngest generations did not appear to have the same concern. I could name hundreds of other businesses that appeared merely from the Web, never having a traditional storefront or traditional business prior to the Internet. For example, eTrade came on the scene and changed the world of stock trading forever. In an effort to catch up, many traditional stockbrokers put up Web sites and added the ability to trade online, but they were competing with a truly online organization and didn't compete well for some time. Many lost significant value, and today the thought of using a stockbroker who doesn't have an online solution is downright ludicrous.

What motivated these IT professionals and businesspeople to build these incredibly dynamic, content-rich, focused, searchable, and efficient sites? The same thing that motivates any businessperson and the same thing that drives them today: satisfaction of a job well done, money, success, and continued investment by businesses in new tools (seen by IT people as toys) for as long as they were having a positive impact on the bottom line and/or the consumer wanted them. As long as those motivations continue to exist in our free market, you can bet your bottom dollar that IT professionals will do everything in their power to create better, faster, and more efficient online services. This means that we will be hired by your competitors to take away your business.

Another incredible force we'll start to see is the partnering of think tanks and scholars throughout the world. While technology used to be relatively isolated with the exception of a few big names, like Sony, that marketed worldwide, today that is becoming less the case. Universities are partnering with other scholars on different continents now, creating an even more rapid advancement of the technological shift we've seen in the past decade. This level of sharing is going to set a new threshold for the pace of technological growth, far exceeding anything we've seen to date. There is rumor of a so-called "Web v. 2," or Web version 2, the second generation of the Web that will be more powerful than we could have imagined even two years ago. Therefore, we will assume throughout the rest of the book that the advance of technology is a given. Google has incredible ties to the academic community and is working diligently with it to provide knowledge to the average person through the ease of the Internet and straightforward Web solutions.

The low-hanging fruit was the first to go—industries easy to revolutionize like retail stores with traditional brick-and-mortar sites that needed to add additional methods by which to obtain products and stay up-to-date with their direct competitors. Online e-tailing growth is outpacing growth in traditional retailers, and they're feeling the pinch. Some are keeping up by providing additional services and using their well-built reputations to encourage growth on both their Internet and traditional sides of the business, but others are floundering and trying to catch up. If a company does things right, it's far cheaper to sell a product online than in a store. The store requires shelf space, a highly valuable commodity. On the Internet, coupled with the right search tool, products are easily found and can be readily shipped from warehouses or direct from manufacturers.

Next, IT hit industries a bit harder to revolutionize—online stock trading or any business requiring true authentication, beyond the credit card. In the early days of the Internet, it wasn't uncommon for the order information, along with the credit card, to be e-mailed to an order processor who then ran your credit card manually and processed your order just as slowly and inefficiently. The integration of shopping carts and online card-processing companies has changed this, thankfully, to an automated process that has saved time and money for companies, all the while making the transaction more secure for the consumer.

Online banking was slow to catch on, except for those banks investing a lot of development money in research and in the means by which to make systems secure. Finally, we saw the transition of systems much harder and more complicated to change. Travel was one of the first, requiring the integration of a tremendous amount of data all delivered in a usable interface by the average consumer with average knowledge and very little knowledge about travel. In this "era" of Web development, we saw travel industries emerge online and companies begin to disappear.

Next, the real estate industry will feel the pinch of online transactions. Much like other industries that have a complicated set of data and numerous obstacles to successful integration, the real estate industry has to merge several other systems, including online banking, online digital signatures, searching for properties, and MLS data, and the list goes on. This is not an easy process or an uncomplicated task, and we've seen the effect of this based on how slow the process has gone—until now. IT is about to go mainstream with the changes in the real estate industry, and we're seeing the same signs, as technologists, of that breakthrough that we have seen in about every other industry studied. It's only a matter of time and that time is nearing. Rest assured, IT professionals will press on to accomplish the goal—to make the industry faster, more efficient, and completely virtual should the consumer choose it.

ENVIRONMENT, CULTURE, AND GENERATIONAL DIFFERENCES

IT, particularly for Generation X and Generation Y individuals, is changing that need and desire for face-to-face interactions. Entire cohorts of people are just as comfortable with, and comforted by, friends using instant messaging as with a friend at lunch, visible and face-to-face. While this has created a never-seen, truly global environment where a friend on another continent is as close as a friend down the street, it has also created an environment by which large groups of people would prefer spending less time doing mundane things that can be automated and more time doing things to propel their success, help their business, grow their relationships, or do something they enjoy. The demands of life today are greater than they were 20 or 40 years ago, and they're growing at a fairly consistent rate.

This phenomenon has fueled a transformation of many industries to a heavy reliance on the Web, and online banking is a good example of this. While a really good study has not yet been conducted on the comfort level of various generations with Web transactions, we do know from preliminary information that those who have grown up with online transactions are far less uncomfortable with the idea of doing business online, and are happy to do anything to make their lives more efficient. We have seen a great cultural shift in our country toward multitasking, with people in highly demanding jobs that don't ever seem to take a break (thanks to technology) and who need to get more done in a smaller amount of time. Web-based transactions fit this need and allow people to do more, do it better, and do it faster in the same amount of time that a traditional transaction took for less of these benefits. If a bank took away its online-banking, bill-pay, and automation features, you can bet a great percentage of its customers would walk away.

In the early days of online banking, most of the transactions were simple and still required someone to input something manually. Over time and by integrating back-end systems, processes became truly automated and monitored by IT staff rather than by business professionals. Real estate has also seen the early signs of the transformation, as many industries have. A search capability here, a tool there, some additional features over here; and then one day we wake up to a totally transformed system with capabilities beyond our expectations. That is what is occurring today in what many are calling Web v. 2.

CONTRIBUTORY CHANGES IN THE REAL ESTATE INDUSTRY

In a world where the stock market hasn't been so exciting after 9/11 and in a society where individuals are starting to realize what business owners have known for years (the concept of leveraging and its incredible financial prowess), we are beginning to see a revolutionary change in the real estate industry that is also having an impact on real estate professionals. A solid 25 percent of purchases made in real estate today are by individuals who will *not* live in the home once it closes escrow. They're either buying it for a family member (how likely is this?), or they are using it as an investment to supplement or replace other investments. Research shows us that the latter is most often the case.

More than ever, individuals are looking to real estate to provide appreciation and equity for their nest eggs, in many cases even as their means to survive. Until recently, a majority of individuals bought one home or maybe two if they wanted a vacation home somewhere. After a decline in the stock market post–9/11 at the same time that an incredible housing boom was under way and interest rates were at historical lows to help rebound our economy, many individuals or even small businesses turned to real estate to make their investments.

There are a few principles by which real estate investors live. First and foremost, we want to balance appreciation with cash flow. It's tough on a moderate income to pay for mortgages of numerous homes. Therefore, we try to offset this with cash flow, or more important, a positive one. This means that the money coming in for a home exceeds the money going out for a home, including the mortgage payment, taxes, insurance, and in many areas association fees and/or Mello-roos.

Second, investors want to buy in the "next hot area," not the has-been areas that are perceived as overvalued by those of us looking to invest our hard-earned dollars in something more tangible than the stock market. For instance, we stay away from the Las Vegases and the Miami Beaches of the nation and we focus on areas that are still considered undervalued, like Georgetown in Texas or Bullhead City in Arizona.

While the stock market has been perceived by many as unstable and operating at the whim of uneducated folks who aren't looking at numbers to make stock decisions, real estate is a tangible item that people will always need. Our theory is that every family needs a home, but not every family needs more pharmaceuticals from a company that could go under tomorrow because of the next corporate scandal. Therefore, there is a perceived stability in real estate that does not exist today in the stock market for many investors. This is good for real estate professionals, who, if positioned right, could stand to gain considerably from this driving demand.

Finally, one of the steadfast rules of real estate investing is to have enough single-family homes in the portfolio to increase the portfolio's value faster than multiunit homes alone would. This means that a good mix of single-family residences (SFRs), duplexes, triplexes, and fourplexes are very important indicators of the success of our portfolio over the long term and our ability to meet monthly commitments.   A friend and colleague referred to an old Monopoly rule about how many "green houses to red houses" should be in a portfolio, and everyone has their "magic number." One thing is for sure, and that is to build our portfolios and therefore our businesses, our nest eggs, or our ability to buy our own single-family residence in an ideal location, the need to add to the mix of each individual's property list will grow.

To help ensure each of these rules is met, one thing investors must look for, and that's quite arguably more important than anything else, is diversification. Having homes in numerous markets, even while creating property-management headaches, helps ensure that a small bubble burst in one area won't take out an entire portfolio. Investors in the stock market have been doing this for years, balancing portfolios or buying mutual funds that are supposedly already balanced. This simple rule, as applied to our real estate investment purchases, means one really big thing for real estate professionals: We need homes in markets we don't live in. Therefore, we need access to multiple MLSs, not just one regional MLS. We also want full service to make the process less cumbersome, and as unbiased an opinion as we can get regarding a particular property. This builds trust between the investor and the real estate professional and opens the door for a long partnership if handled properly. Are you seeing yet where you might fit into the future picture?

There are new rules in the Internet age, however, and those who don't adhere to them and who try to work with individuals managing properties just the same as they would with their stock portfolios will not be successful with this growing and important sector of clients. For investors, one thing has held true throughout the past decades and that is the importance of leveraging. Many of you reading this book might be new real estate professionals or even seasoned ones who have moved through your careers with MLS books and pages of documentation. You don't really know where to begin in terms of adding technology or how to really understand what's out there and what you need to do.

The National Association of Realtors® offers a course developed purely online in conjunction with Internet Crusade called the e-PRO Technology Certification Program. e-PRO is a certification that does more than add more acronyms to the end of your name (though it does that too); this is a program that was created by Realtors® for Realtors®. Taking the course and becoming e-PRO certified is something to consider before taking the leap of adding technology to your repertoire of competitive advantages.

We've established well in this book that the way you do business is going to change due to technology. Reading this book is one way to prepare; reading others books on real estate technology (such as *The Real Estate Technology Guide* by Klein, Reilly, and Barnett, 2003) will also be of assistance. But if you want to take it a step further, check out *www.e-PROnar.com*—the Certification for Internet Professionalism.

Some of the many topics you will cover in the e-PRO course include:

- Understanding the Internet and key skills
- Steps to becoming an e-PRO
- Surviving the challenge by making the technology investment
- Recognizing expectations of your connected customer base
- Joining online communities, chat forums, and listservs—all tools you can use yourself to build your community

- Computing fundamentals, including connectivity choices, free Internet services, Windows familiarity, and shopping online
- History and structure of the internet, including domain names, the importance of owning and controlling second level domains, and the integration of Internet marketing into conventional strategies
- Internet hosting, including what it does, why it's important, and whom to choose to do it
- Electronic mail communications and marketing tips, including effective uses of email, the benefits of incorporating e-mail into your plan, managing e-mail effectively, mail services, and other e-mail tips that go further into the use of attachments, HTML, etc., in messages
- Important Web sites today and the future uses of tomorrow; personal Web site options, Webmasters and Web designers, creating an online presence, blogging, content and design, and Internet Web marketing strategies
- Creating virtual communities in the new global economy, the power of communities, community do's and don'ts, prospecting on the Internet, and finding leads while maintaining existing and new relationships
- Using tools of the trade—everything from digital cameras to using your personal digital assistant (PDA)

Finally, the all-online course ties everything you've learned together to help you create a seamless online community that generates leads, helps you sell, and becomes a place for prospects and existing clients to go—all while teaching you the best practices specific to your industry. The course also may count towards your continuing education credit. Visit the link at *www.e-PROnar.com* under CE approval for more information.

Whether you are a seasoned professional looking to add technology to your business or a newbie who has a grip on technology but not its application to real estate, this is a certification program worth looking into. You can take the course at your own pace (you have six months to complete it), and work entirely on-line. If clients want to find someone specific to their needs (such as someone who will use the Internet to communicate with them more frequently than traditional methods), they may look for someone with this certification, and if one of your strategies is to use technology to beat online competition, this is one great opportunity for you. The course focuses on Internet use, not what to buy or gadgets you need to have. The current cost of the course is $359; if you are not a realtor the cost is $459.

WHAT CAN A REAL ESTATE PROFESSIONAL DO? FINDING YOUR NICHE

We've talked about cultural and environmental changes, other similar industries, interest in real estate as a replacement for traditional investments like the stock market, generational differences between those who currently own real estate and those who are about to own, a history and motivational review of the IT world, and the need for an adaptation to a changing economy. But, given all these massive and important changes, what can a real estate professional do about it? The ideas behind the suggestions for solidifying business in the years to come are from IT theory applied to real estate, what I have found in consulting with organizations, and studying other industries.

The study of those who have survived in rapid market changes and those who haven't helps shed some light on general issues that real estate professionals need to be concerned with for their future success. First and foremost, I encourage each of you to ask yourself the following questions. These are questions I ask my clients when they are looking to strategize on how their business model should look to survive the rapid change about to occur in real estate.

- What am I the best at? In a world of specialists and niches, everyone needs to be really good at something. Ask yourself what that something *currently* is, which will help you determine a starting point at something you can be exceptional at.

- Where have most of my clients come from? Are they coming from referrals? Are they coming from the Internet? How can I find out if I don't know already?
- How am I currently advertising? How many new clients do I get each month from each form of advertising? What is the cost of each type of advertising?
- Which is the best "bang for the buck" marketing approach when trying to get new listings?
- Do I provide a method by which my clients can give me feedback anonymously? If not, why not?
- Am I partnered with a technology company that can provide insight into the future of IT and the direction it is headed and not to just the current available systems? In other words, do I have a strategic IT partner or just an outsourced help-desk person(s)?
- If you are an independent: How do I plan to grow my business when Web-based transactions are more common? Am I set up to provide wire transfers, e-mail communications, MLS searches, and investor information via the Internet? Have I reviewed the new criteria required for organizations who wish to do business online?
- If you work for a company: What tools is my company providing for me to be successful? Does it have a strategic IT vision? If so, what is it and how can I jump on board? If not, am I sure I am with the right organization or is it too short-sighted to ensure my long-term success?
- What are the greatest changes I've seen in the demographics of my clients (buyers and sellers) in the past five years since the Internet expanded rapidly? How do I expect this to change and what makes me think so? (Remember each area and market may be different.)
- What do my clients ask for the most from me? The least? Does a certain type of buyer tend to fit one of the require-

ments most often? In other words, does a small family buying their first home tend to want more phone calls while a
successful investor wants to be contacted by e-mail only?
Have I determined what appeals to each segment and how
I can customize my communications to each group of individuals or businesses?

- In what ways am I leveraging and managing strategic partnerships? Do I have them and how are they benefiting me?
Beyond the immediate dollar, are they providing any long-
term substantial benefit? Have they agreed to keep up with
the technology I begin to explore?
- How can I make myself most useful to my clients? (Try to
think beyond the obvious when answering this question.)
What do they really want from me and, most important,
how can I provide it to them?
- Which part of my job have I loved? Which have I not been
so sold on? Do the parts I love have a place in the Internet
era?

After writing down the answer to each of these, reread them
as you focus on the section of the book that follows. This may help
you gain a sense of purpose and excitement as you proceed toward what is guaranteed to be an exciting time in real estate.
There may be many solutions to this opportunity for growth, but
these should help get you on the right track and provide some
food for thought as you determine what you should be doing to
make sure you are ready for what is about to come—not to mention what's already here. Remember, none of these ideas are
proven strategies, but they are based on experienced advice and
sound business practice.

REINVENTING YOUR VALUE

One of the fastest and most successful strategies in maintaining or increasing momentum in any changing market is to make

you and your business invaluable to the consumer. Whether this is proving to your boss at your day job that you are essential to your company's growth (for instance, if you work for a real estate agency or a bank), or proving to your clients that you have what it takes, the underlying motivation is the same. Your company and your clients must know that without you, they will have a much harder time being successful.

This sounds easy enough, and may even at first thought sound overly simplistic. Think back to what you answered to the previous questions. How do you make yourself more useful than the next professional? If everyone has the same competition and similar practices, how can you differentiate yourself? Think beyond "I answer my e-mail faster" and think about adding *value*. Company executives often ask, "Does this task or product or service add value?" If the answer is no, then the effort is not made or the product is removed from the product lineup. They may do a SWOT analysis—analyzing their Strengths, Weaknesses, Opportunities, and Threats—and then try to mitigate the threats while capitalizing on their opportunities.

The same rules apply to any industry touched by the Internet, especially those about to be inundated. You have to determine what value you add above and beyond technology and try to stay in touch with the human element if you wish to go that route. Now imagine that the human element is less required in the new age, and ask yourself what value you add then. If you can't answer that question and don't add value behind the scenes for those doing the work, then I advise that you spend some more time thinking about this. Imagine all of the possibilities—providing online data others don't; lowering your commissions substantially for clients who choose to use efficient communication means. The possibilities are endless! You may even decide to become an online provider of information and even open your own online shop competing with your colleagues.

In the travel industry, many agents survived by making themselves useful to businesses for a small fee. They turned to quantity and not quality and their businesses survived because of the volume of people they served. That isn't necessarily bad; they adapted to the business need of saving costs, and added value to the service by negotiating contracts with hotel chains and rental-car agencies on behalf of their clients. They created single-billing for companies with a lot of traveling employees and began giving credits for change fees airlines charged. These are all ways they added value to the Expedia and Travelocity sites of the world, and you have them in your industry, too. What if you gave your investors a spreadsheet each month with the value of their properties (which you can get online easily), along with their growth rate and then make suggestions for them to improve their equity position and cash flow? Your investors would love you!

Travel agents had to think outside of the box and do things that went against their usual method of operating; ultimately, they were able to build new partnerships and relationships while learning to compete in a new Internet-based market. Less than the ideal number survived, but the efforts of those who have will serve as a springboard for professionals in other industries about to face the same turmoil. Remember, you are not alone in real estate, for many industries have been affected by such advances in technology. More important, remember it's the goal of the technologist to build something so creative, so unique, and so integrative that you are out of a job. Don't let that happen!

Many of the flat-fee companies and low-cost brokers need partners too! We've talked about some of the ways travel agents successfully navigated the move to online business models. One of them was to join the guys who are already focusing their business model for the online environment. In some cases, this may mean giving up your business; in other cases, it means a terrific potential partnership!

One such site gaining incredible momentum and one you need to look at is PropertyGuys.com. PropertyGuys.com helps buyers and sellers together avoid the high cost of a middleman. It charges sellers a flat fee up front and charges no commission on the sale. I realize this, on the surface, appears like it is only direct competition. However, in order to be successful, the founders of this site actually partner with real estate professionals, including legal and title, real estate agents, and mortgage brokers, to provide a one-stop shop for their clients. The benefit to consumers is obvious and important for you to notice because this is an example of your competition! The system gives the seller the ultimate control over their home sale process and benefit from a system that lets them pick and choose which services they require and how much they are willing to pay agents.

For those with some foresight in the real estate industry, this could be an incredible way for you to align with the new marketplace. Agents benefit from online traffic that lets them reach more qualified buyers. Specific marketing packages are set up for each consumer, and they often include agents. This portion of the business is given over to partner agents, which could be you or your organization. For more information, visit *www.propertyguys.com*.

RETHINK YOUR MARKETING CAMPAIGN

When analyzing your answers to the questions asked in the previous section, what stands out most about your marketing campaign? How is the marketing method you use different from that of your competitors? How are you going to change it when your competitors aren't just your neighboring real estate professionals but Web sites that offer seamless transactions all with the click of a mouse? Once you know how you'll add value, how will you communicate that message to your potential clients? A great product is nothing if no one knows about it. When purely Web-based competition comes on the horizon, it will start off slowly and pick up momentum as the new generation of Web users become homeowners and/or real estate investors.

When this occurs, the strategy must be thought through once again and modified. In fact, you may need to update your strategy every six months to one year because technology is changing that rapidly. One critical element is understanding the environment in which the clients exist and understanding their nature. The new breed of owners and investors will not be afraid of handling a transaction themselves. They will have seen their parents and/ or peers do this and look at it as any other investor or online purchase. Many believed no one would ever trade a stock online, either; that was then, this is now. This Web-friendliness and comfort level with the Internet will create an entirely new breed of consumer—consumers who will grow steadily until they become the majority. Every theoretical and practical application implicates that this paradigm shift will occur, and technologists are feverishly trying to be the first ones to implement it.

Ask yourself:

- How will I compete with the marketing capability of a venture capitalist–backed technology company? A founder of a major corporation left his post and started a company in Southern California to provide low-cost and flat-rate commissions to sellers. How will I compete with people like him?

- How will I provide investors with intelligent information? If this is going to be your niche market, you need to understand what they want from you.

- How will I provide multiple regions of MLS listings to my clients? Do I need new partnerships? Do I need to be licensed elsewhere or work for a firm that can get me the data I need to expand my service areas?

- How will I make myself known in a world inundated by real estate professionals that will grow to almost purely Web-based professionals?

- Do I want to focus on the investor market or the primary-residence market? How will I focus my efforts on that particular group of individuals or should I take a shotgun approach and try to attract them all?

UNDERSTANDING THE NEXT GENERATION OF HOMEBUYERS

It's always tough to predict what a new generation will demand out of life, what their culture will be like, and how they will define happiness and the American dream. By reviewing the way the thoughts and experiences of one generation differ from others and by interviewing those who are living it firsthand, we can begin to see some patterns that are developing that will be useful in setting the stage for the future.

Today's youth will be tomorrow's homebuyers and homesellers. Today's educated college graduates are already purchasing homes despite record high prices—partly because their parents, the boomers, are selling and making a lot of money. Who doesn't want to be in on that action? With a new set of mortgage possibilities available to the average homebuyer, it's no wonder individuals who just three years ago would not qualify for an apartment much less a mortgage do so rather easily today. Some of the mortgage options that have shaped the industry include the negative amortization or reverse mortgage; the interest-only three-, five-, and seven-year adjustable mortgages; and the pay-option adjustable-rate mortgages. One perfectly clear element is that younger generations want someone who is educated in a variety of the buying and selling requirements, including mortgages.

Understanding each option or at least knowing the pros and cons of the various types is one way to offer a competitive advantage to your clients. Essentially, you have to know more than just your own business, but the value you will add to the transaction will help sustain your career momentum and position you well for Internet competitiveness. This list by no means provides all the details nor is it an exhaustive list of the pros and cons you should be aware of, but it does note three types of mortgages that are hot with the younger crowd that you should understand and be familiar with. You can look up each of these on the Internet or talk with mortgage brokers or lenders to understand each organization's specific loan program.

The reverse mortgage or negative amortization mortgage lets the homeowner add to the principal balance of the home loan by not paying all the interest, essentially deferring it to another date. While on the surface this doesn't seem like a wise idea, many consumers are finding that if they invest the money they are adding to their mortgage or use it to pay down other higher-interest debts, they come out ahead of the game year after year and can afford more house on top of it. Make no mistake that this loan choice is most popular with younger generations who see themselves moving several more times before "settling" into a home or who view homes as investments. They may also want to provide a more lavish home for their family while living on income fixed by their jobs. With real estate appreciating in most markets at record-setting rates, it's been a no-brainer for many in these high-appreciation areas to use negative amortization loans to afford a home, offer flexibility, and make more money for little cost. You should be really clear on the pros and cons of reverse mortgages and either explain them to clients or refer clients to someone who can.

Reverse mortgages offer several pros, including the ability to get into a higher-priced home, to take advantage of fast-moving appreciation in a higher-value home that will see greater return, to anticipate job-related income and predict what type of house one can afford in the future, and to invest money saved by deferring interest in investments with higher rates of return. Cons include some level of instability (this is not your grandfather's fixed mortgage, though payment and interest caps help offset some risk) and the all-important but often overlooked fact that many lenders offering home equity lines of credit (HELOCs) do not like to take a "second position" behind a negative-amortization primary loan (neg-am primary).

Banks become concerned that the owner will defer interest and the home value will decrease, and if the buyer were to go into foreclosure, the bank in the second position would not be paid because there wouldn't be enough equity in the home. Most banks that will secure a HELOC behind a neg-am primary do so at higher rates (almost never prime or prime minus some portion of points), and the bank assumes the owner maxes the loan out at max negative value (often 125 percent), thereby lending less than the usual 80 percent or 90 percent combined loan to value (CLTV). Banks are most secure when they assume worst-possible scenarios, so even though a buyer's loan balance may be $1,000,000, the bank may assume that the owner will maximize the negative amortization of 125 percent and that the balance is really $1,250,000 or some variation in between. Certainly, buyers can still get these loans, but they come at a hefty price. This has a great impact on the ability to secure equity lines quickly and easily. This should be clearly explained to any homebuyer, and again understanding this will help secure your future in the marketplace.

Those of you who are not mortgage professionals need to partner with someone who is and who fully understands options available to your clients. I recall my first experience working with an agent; I was making a good salary and looking for a home to move into from my apartment. The real estate agent in the area I was looking told me I could not afford more than a $125,000 house. I thought, $125,000 in south Orange County!? Good luck! After looking at many one-bedroom run-down town houses, I went directly to a lender at Washington Mutual who, over the phone, said something like "Dani, you are crazy. You can easily afford $220,000." Now we were talking! I could buy a brand-new home and even a few upgrades. Of course, this isn't the case in the area anymore, but the real estate agent, not aware of what was really needed to qualify a buyer, sent me in the wrong direction. What happened as a result? I went to John Laing Homes, a homebuilder in my area, and bought a brand-new house that doubled in value in five years, and the real estate agent lost out on a potentially good deal. Be aware of what is out there and what your buyers will qualify for, because they look to you to be experts. Admit what you don't know, and send your clients to those who do.

The three-, five-, or seven-year interest-only adjustable-rate mortgages (ARMs) lock in a rate for the aforementioned three, five, or seven years and then adjust after that to a particular index or moving average. This is popular with individuals who want to pay only the interest on their homes, and see their equity building as a result of appreciation rather than paying down their mortgage. This is another huge difference in generations. Younger generations don't fear "never owning their home"; in fact, the average person moves every five to seven years, so paying down the loan by a few thousand dollars is really irrelevant to this crowd. Understanding this is critical to helping this generation of individuals.

The benefits of this type of loan include paying only the interest and not going negative on the balance but not paying more than you have to, either. Benefits also include a lower monthly payment and usually lower interest rates than with fixed-term and fixed-rate loans. In fact, fewer loans today are traditional fixed-rate loans than ever before in history. This trend will only continue as banks find creative ways to create win-win situations for homeowners and their shareholders. Cons to this type of loan include a short fixed-payment period, so the payment will adjust (although payment and interest-rate caps usually apply) after the initial fixed period. If the rates go up substantially, a segment of the population will find themselves paying much higher mortgage payments than in the fixed years of the loan. The same con applies to those in the negative-amortization loans or reverse mortgages. This may be a good middle ground between those who want low payments but don't want to add to their balance each month, and those who want the ease of pulling equity out of their homes quickly.

The pay-option adjustable-rate mortgage, or pay-option ARM, is essentially a negative-amortization loan with a few added flexible payment options. This type of loan gives the homeowners several options regarding payments each month. The options include neg-am (deferring interest) for the lowest payment, interest only (not paying down the principle but not adding to the balance), 30-year fixed payoffs (paying the amount that would be required if you wanted to own your home in 30 years), or 15-year fixed payoffs (paying the amount that would be required if you wanted to own your home in 15 years).

While many younger people like this flexibility because their income often is also flexible or changes (this is especially true for those who are self-employed or in the sales professions), many older people consider it too risky because it's easy to defer interest and add to the balance each month. As discussed earlier, there are two drastically differing viewpoints on the upsides and downsides of deferring interest. This type of loan is very popular among those who want to have the flexibility of investing the money that would go to paying down their mortgage in other leveraged investments (such as additional real estate). Therefore, this type of loan needs to be clearly understood and explained to real estate clients.

The preference of loan types and the willingness to take risks is one of many differences in generations when it comes to buying and selling homes. As nonscientific interviews with those who buy and sell homes as primary residences and investment property revealed, there are generalities that hold true among the new Internet-savvy generation. These include:

- Greater willingness to shop around online because of a comfort level and an understanding of technology that surpasses any previous generation, and demand for price comparisons and for those selling services or products to know about their competitors' offerings.
- Internet-savvy generations are quite used to tools such as bottomdollar.com and PriceGrabber.com that instantly compare the costs of products including shipping and potential taxes. This same method will apply to real estate in the future.
- A do-it-yourself attitude when thousands of dollars are at stake (as in the sale of a home through an agent or by owner); even more so with high home prices that we see today.

- A desire to sell to or buy from other Internet-savvy people—
there is a general comfort with others who are also comfortable with technology. They tend to be less paranoid about
completing transactions and about communicating quickly
and efficiently through electronic means. A personal example: I described earlier in the book an agent who wasn't
communicating well. I was referred to another agent (again
I am using one because I don't live in the area I'm selling a
home in) who is extremely communicative and e-mails regularly, and my perception of her is far greater even if the
previous agent is actually a better real estate professional.
Even though the house is still moving slowly, the agent
makes all the difference.
- A very busy schedule—these Internet-friendly people are often extremely busy and look to the most efficient process
possible to complete a task or transaction. Often they are
entrepreneurs and work more hours or multitask multiple
jobs and investment opportunities and they want speed and
the ability to do things online where possible.
- They take advantage of tax laws and understand them better than previous generations. Thanks to the Internet making tax laws and changes more transparent and forums to
share investment and tax-reduction ideas (even the IRS has
jumped on board), the Internet-savvy generations are more
likely to know their options when it comes to exchanging
property (known as 1031s for the name of the tax code the
exchanges represent), and often handle their own taxes
with tax software.

The younger generations have an overwhelming positive attitude about their future and about the state of the economy. This
has been proven in study after study. This positive attitude encourages them to take more risks and to leverage a considerable
amount of their investment, and it makes them prime targets for
the sale of your services. Because they're getting into the market
earlier, they are also spending more and don't have the same pre-

vious bad experiences haunting them. Case in point: After completing several transactions almost entirely online this past year, I advised my mother, who is a few years shy of the boomer category, on the sale of her house without using an agent. I advised her to do this because her only retirement savings is in her primary residence, and she cannot afford to pay $50,000 or more in commissions. After a buyer came to her with a cash offer, she took the deal. However, her panic throughout the entire transaction was obvious and overwhelming at times. She worried about small details that those of us with a trust in the process and knowledge of computer systems take for granted. This was not her first home sale, and she'd purchased and sold other properties. Still her panic was notable. Younger generations don't worry whether the ATM will credit their deposits, whether returns will fund to their credit card, or whether they need to hang onto sales slips; they just inherently trust technology more than older folks do. These older folks are excellent demographics for you to boost your business! These are the folks that the old methods of selling still work for. But they won't be around forever. Perhaps you only want to be in real estate for another decade or so, so you specialize in low-fee sales for boomers looking to retire to other areas. I'll discuss this in greater detail—it is certainly a hot opportunity! Keep in mind that those in older generations indicate that young people take excessive risk, and note that the younger generations had not seen great poverty such as those who lived through the Great Depression and its long-lived aftermath. Those in older generational groups generally regard the younger generation as having a naive approach and viewpoint with regard to their financial outlook.

Younger people are saving early thanks to 401(k) accounts readily available by their companies and are saving more of their money at younger ages than previous generations. They don't believe Social Security will be around long enough to be of any use to them, so they have taken matters into their own hands and assume they will have zero money from Social Security. Many want real estate to be a part of this transition.

People belonging to older generations are less willing to take risk by default, partially because they have less time for market corrections before needing their retirement money. Those in younger generations know they have time for recovery if the economy heads south, and take more risk accordingly.

Another common desire by those in the younger generation cohort is a desire to complete transactions online where possible, freeing them up to do other things. Online banking has proved this point for the past few years by providing more and more services online and seeing the tremendous result—these generations are using the system and they're trusting it while it isn't as easily adopted by older generations.

This brings us to another common thread—a trust in the systems they often helped develop. It isn't only the IT crowd that is willing to use technology in place of traditional means while trusting implicitly the integrity of the system. Studies have shown they worry less about identity theft because they spent their late teen years and early adulthood with credit card companies that readily protect consumers and investigate fraud on their behalf. Teenagers and young adults grew up using eBay to buy goods from others, and understand the responsibility and usefulness of peer feedback. Other than the hassle that comes along with straightening out the "mess," younger generations are more confident that the issues will ultimately be straightened out and handled, and because their family obligations in general are being delayed until later in life, it isn't so big a deal for them to lose their investments and have to restart again. This greater confidence creates an environment by which they prefer online transactions to paper-based ones.

Traditional scare tactics don't work on investors and even on many casual homebuyers and homesellers. We aren't afraid of holding an open house or even putting our lockbox combination on someone's Web site if we believe they are relatively secure, and we certainly aren't afraid of signing some paperwork. In fact, half the time we may not read beyond the check boxes and we'll still do just fine, only finding out at the close of escrow that we had agreed to something we didn't realize. No big deal, we move on and we adjust. Chances are this isn't our only or last home, and we may not even be living in it ever. Our attachment to the process and to the home doesn't require another human to intervene.

On a personal note, while studying this particular phenomenon, I couldn't help but think of my Grandfather Don, who at one point, would have called me crazy for leveraging my primary residence to the max and using the money to invest in real estate all over the country, trusting property managers to handle my affairs and often dumping my own personal income into my business mortgage payment accounts just to pay my monthly obligations on homes in areas I have no guarantee will appreciate and in some cases, don't even know what the homes look like much less who lives in them. While he'd far prefer traditional investments and I know deep down he believes this is a potential "get rich quick" scheme brought about by my lack of seeing poverty and great real estate depreciation in my lifetime, those who are business colleagues and friends doing the same thing have a different viewpoint. We are no longer the minority; even popular newsmagazines are filled with articles about common people earning a modest wage who made hundreds of thousands of dollars doing exactly what many of us are doing today. Is it a riskier time to do so? Probably. Is it worth it? Definitely. Are we a great market for you? Maybe the best of all.

We believe that the concept of leveraging is our best bet to an early retirement, and although it creates a stressful, tapped-out lifestyle in the short term, eventually our sacrifices and hard work will pay off. Often we track our net worth in spreadsheets and financial tools, and as we watch our eggs grow we know we're that much closer to "retirement" (aka doing something other than our day jobs) at 40—sooner if we're lucky. We rely on the Internet and technology to give us data we need to make our investments as secure as we can and with as much confidence as we can in a market many are calling "the worst bubble since the 1980s," a time I vaguely remember. Perhaps Grandfather is right, but my colleagues and I will keep following our dreams and putting into practice what we studied in economics classes and in finance classes, not trusting anyone to take care of us but ourselves. There is a sense of pride in building a business like this, and although it grows slowly, it almost always does grow. We are more prone to risk taking, and we demand competence and integrity in the marketplace—something that is becoming less common if you ask many of us who are used to immediate responses and constant communication and expect it from our business partners. In fact, at some point a person becomes numb to the fact that money isn't there to close escrow; you just figure it out and make it happen. In fact, there's very little time to worry when things go our way and are done fast.

Our elders saw a different way of living and experienced a different hardship; they saw their parents with a 25 percent to 50 percent chance of unemployment and saw great suffering, average workers and their children begging on the streets, and complete financial ruin. The younger generation's worst fears are the 11 percent to 15 percent interest rates seen in the 1980s with a handful of variable-rate mortgages hitting their three-, five-, or seven-year mark. If that's the worst case, we'll take it. Granted it may not be, but that's our perception. If you can help us figure out how to mitigate risk while still running our lives at our fast pace, we'll listen to you all the way to the bank.

Understanding this mentality is critical to successfully working with new generations who are more educated, thanks in part to the readily available array of information that's easily searchable and reliable. Real estate professionals—start asking your younger clients what they want and what they expect. Ask them what their worries are, and compare that to those buyers and sellers you represent or work with who are from older generations. This change is critical to the survival of real estate professionals in the new century. To the grandfathers all over the world worrying about your grandchildren and their crazy investment schemes—it's okay; we'll either make it big and retire in comfort, or learn the art of suffering just as you did but in our own way. Either way, we'll be all right, but we do appreciate your concern.

BABY BOOMER TIME

In the previous section, I mentioned the baby boomers. I've given this suggestion a lot of thought, and I believe many of you may like this idea. We know you need a new strategy, preferably one with a niche. Consider this: We know that baby boomers are moving at an astronomical, unforeseen rate. We know they are cashing out of their suburban and urban areas and moving to places like Arizona and Florida. Consider representing them—exclusively. This would work for real estate agents, mortgage brokers, and lenders. What if you were experts in the baby boomer move? You help them sell their homes, help them find hot areas for their generation of adult active-living requirements, and handle their entire transaction while taking into consideration all their financial needs. Surely, you could find a way to capitalize on this incredibly growing market and trend—handling financial affairs as a boomer expert does not require technological savviness.

WEB BASED VERSUS WEB ENABLED

Don't just add online services or enhance them—build them! If you don't have the revenue or income to build your own, partner with companies who have them readily available. Some companies will even sell you an entire solution ready to go on your site that lets people find homes, put them on a wish list, and send it to you along with their prequalification information. A hint on where to find them: Talk to your title and escrow companies. They are usually the ones who know.

In previous chapters, we discussed in rather great length the movement from Web-based environments to Web-enabled environments. Essentially, what this means is that technology is gradually moving all industries from offering some enhanced services online or easy communications via e-mail to being purely Web based, meaning the entire transaction is handled online. Think of the scenario mentioned in this chapter regarding a theoretical online transaction. That scenario isn't a pipe dream; it is in the works, and many companies are partnering together to make it happen. You can either enjoy the ride until then and change careers (or take a drastic hit in income), or put together a plan to embrace Web enablement and even offer it yourself.

Real estate professionals working for companies may have a tough time understanding this, and those of you in this boat are somewhat at the mercy of your organizations with regard to your ability to adapt to the future. But it's clear that if your company isn't partnering with organizations that will offer Web-based solutions in the future, you may want to consider changing companies or going independent and just working for a broker—or even becoming one yourself. Many larger companies may have in-house staff or outsourced organizations working diligently on putting together the latest and greatest solution. If this "solution" doesn't embrace technology at levels not seen before, don't count on it having an impact. Creating clicks to e-mail links on a Web page *does not count,* and neither does creating links to other companies' Web sites. The next generation of technology is all about integration, and it's occurring at the deepest technological levels imaginable. For instance, your system needs to be able to electronically send paperwork to title and escrow, to lenders, make comparisons, and let the client access the status of his or her file. This is just the beginning.

In the scenario outlined in this chapter, one of the underlying premises was the ability for disparate systems to communicate, including those belonging to entirely different organizations. Think lenders, appraisers, title companies, escrow companies, inspectors, even the termite people all connecting into one system and sharing information, being updated electronically on tasks still needing completion, and then sending the entire package for e-signing to the client through digitally secure software. This is going on behind the scenes at a steady pace, and once this portion is complete, many companies will be able to "go live" with online transaction processing.

A word of advice—enhancing is fine for now, but it won't be soon. Think new systems, think integration, and your world will be a happier place in 2007 and beyond. Find out if the escrow and title companies you routinely work with offer online back-end communications. If they do, talk with Web developers or Web-development companies who may be able to enable your system to talk to the third-party systems. Use your imagination and develop a system by which your customers can handle their transactions from the cradle to the grave without ever speaking with an individual if they so choose.

Web-enhancing ideas you may be able to easily incorporate into your Web site today include (these are the minimum for today, not what is needed for tomorrow):

- Online mortgage calculators that display payment information alongside the MLS search results based on mortgage preferences and credit scores, all with a guide on what it means.
- Expanded MLS search offerings into other areas—while this may require licensing changes and registration fees, it may help you market yourself a bit differently and expand your service area.
- Referrals for online applications to lenders who are integrated with the interest in a particular property.
- Customized feedback and communication based on the consumer's selection of information he or she wishes to receive (or, more important, not receive).
- Marketing and Web applications that will funnel information about who is visiting your site and what they're looking at, all while managing these leads into a sales funnel you can work with that reports data automatically to those who need to know about it.

- Online brochures featuring not only MLS data but information put together from demographic material, including rental comps, appreciation in that area, employment and income rates, etc., that are downloadable and offer plenty of ways to contact you or your company for more information.
- Pay to have your site come up more often and higher on search engine results, particularly for the areas you serve.
- Offer answers to frequently asked questions commonly known online as FAQs; include sections on mortgages, appreciation in the markets you work in, and maybe even other experts they can call. Update this often with questions that come in from your Web site. Consider checking into an online forum and addressing your clients' questions. Give them a space where the one thing they have in common—using you as a service provider—keeps them connected.
- Give your customers a place to speak with one another, a place to connect and a forum in which to share ideas. Regularly check the forum, and provide your expertise on the topics and questions presented. This makes you a part of their community rather than just a vendor supplying them with houses.
- Respond the way you were approached. In other words, if someone sends you an e-mail or submits a Web form, be sure to include a question about how the person would like to be contacted—e-mail or phone. Include a best time to call for those preferring it, and then be sure to hit that time frame within a few minutes. You don't have to look overly eager, but expect your client is extremely busy and probably juggling several things at once. If they just e-mailed you, it means they may have five minutes to spare right now—and right now is a good time to call or e-mail them back. Note the time your client is regularly available in a file somewhere, and then refer to it when you want to get in touch with them. Avoid phone tag—e-mail is better. Phone tag just

adds to their to-do lists, and they may already feel inundated.

- If a potential client or existing customer asks to be communicated with by e-mail, don't spam them (spam is sending unsolicited or excessive e-mail). Send an e-mail introducing yourself or addressing that particular question with *very brief* marketing information about yourself or your company. Skip this step if he or she is already a client. If someone just e-mails you, e-mail them back with answers to his or her questions. Don't respond to his or her e-mail with a phone call; this is nothing short of annoying, particularly with younger people. We have organizational methods built into our e-mail systems, and we expect you to respect that. Doing so will encourage mutual respect while responding promptly helps build the relationship. This also shows you actually use the technology that you put out there and aren't afraid of it. Chances are, if the client found you this way, he or she isn't, either.

PARTNER WITH THE BIG GUYS?

Concluding that you can't be good at everything is easy when you crunch the numbers and take a hard look at your job and where your time is spent. The question is, do you need to be good at everything? If you can't find a niche, or you don't want to find a niche, consider partnering with the big guys who may not need one. Do what many travel agents did—pair up with companies to provide a value-added service. Expedia.com doesn't just compete with agents; it actually hired many of them. Where else would it get an educated workforce? While at first you might feel like a sellout, you might actually be one of the few still in the industry five years from now. In fact, many of the travel professionals outplaced by online travel companies were hired back as experts. I am not referring to call centers often housed in India or other countries where contract, educated labor is cheap, but experts who put together packages and work the business side of the house, address customer concerns, or offer advice through online forums or by phone.

The business-to-business market is hotter than ever within the travel industry. In the "old days" (pre-Web-enablement days), businesses often chose one travel agency to handle their transactions and billed them accordingly. Often the fees were modest and there were some markups on various transactions. Today, while many of these companies still exist and have contracts, the terms of those contracts are vastly different. Instead, many have partnerships with online travel companies that provide company accounts to their employees to book their travel and even obtain online approval through their systems connected to their clients' electronic mail system. Those who couldn't "beat them joined them," to use the old cliché. Many went to work for the very companies that helped create an environment in which they lost their jobs or their businesses. They became travel experts for these companies or travel consultants for private individuals or organizations, where their expertise was still valued but the role they played changed substantially.

The same options are available today for real estate professionals. Seek and contact the companies that are embracing Web enablement. Find professional organizations that are encouraging partnerships and join them. Look to the standards organizations who are determining what the new standards for online transactions will be, and be a part of the process. Figure out where you see yourself in the future—do you want to specialize in a particular area? If so, find those companies that are best positioned to help you and begin creating your partnerships now. You may not have to join them entirely, but imagine an entirely different career. Much like the travel agent, think, perhaps, of becoming a professional real estate consultant working for yourself and representing your clients not in their transactions but as an individual reviewing contracts and handling some of the paperwork for relatively low fees. The possibilities are endless, but a creative imagination is important. If you don't want to lose the entrepreneurial aspect of your job, then joining the big guys probably won't be for you. The key here is to determine what you do best and then maximize that. The Web-based future is all about specialists and key players who can be relied on for their expertise and their embracing of technology.

In addition to partnering with the big guys, some real estate professionals are going to work for them. For example, many of the bigger organizations online, like ZipRealty, may put their agents on salary and remove the financial incentive to close the next deal. The marketing department handles lead generation, and experts are hired to be of assistance to homebuyers or home-sellers if they need advice. However, they are essentially salaried employees working for the organization rather than independent business owners.

Lets look at a few companies you might consider partnering with. There are several companies out there that can help in different aspects of your quest for technology innovation as a real estate professional. GURU Networks is one of them.

GURU Networks offers consulting and technology services for the residential real estate industry in particular, which means you're not competing against large commercial real estate companies. Among the consulting offerings are network design and implementation, monitoring and management, security services to protect your network and the attached servers and workstations, due diligence studies, RFP creation and response evaluation, even office layout design to reduce your cost per agent! This is only the consulting side.

Take a look at their product offerings online, among which is an Enterprise Solution that provides one central database with all of the data and functions needed to run a brokerage. So what does this do for you? It provides a full personnel system, with pay plans and measurements; leads management, including source of business reporting; transaction management; document creation and management; disbursement and interface to accounting system for automatic posting of disbursement entries; and an option for a complete reporting system. The company also provides a full IDX Web site with property search as well as separate Web pages for each office and agent, populated from their database, eliminating the need for a Webmaster! You might even find many of your team members are freed up to do other tasks, saving you more than the cost of implementing the system. (We all look for positive ROI, right?)

Of course you'll want to know what advantages their systems offer your customers. Your clients have full visibility over the status of their transaction from first search or listing of the property through the settlement, over a secure Web site they can access 24 hours a day.

This organization has many solutions to offer. Partnering with organizations like this is a fast-track to being Web-enabled and providing high technology to your clients. If you'd like to learn more, visit GURU Networks on the Internet at *www.gurunet.net,* phone 888-487-8638, or e-mail *info@gurunet.net*

Believe it or not, there are organizations that will help both the consumer and the agent! Agents may consider partnering with these organizations to increase their sales; yet consumers will get a competitive bid.

This type of business model is similar to that of eBay or eLoans. Just as these organizations list an item up for auction and allow buyers to bid, RealtyBaron.com allows sellers to list their home as available and lets agents bid on the commission and other details. Homeowners and realtors anonymously negotiate sales-related services. Once the bidding is complete, the winning realtor and homeowner are introduced via e-mail. RealtyBaron.com only receives a service fee after closing if the lead resulted in a sale for the realtor. This protects you, the real estate professional, from paying for leads that don't generate anything.

Let's walk through a typical scenario. A seller lists his/her home on the Web site. The homeowner remains anonymous, protecting him- or herself from someone banging on their door or calling to solicit business. The model includes something often overlooked but vitally important called AgentRank™. A detailed description of this is available at *www.realtybaron.com/agentrank.*

Much like eBay's feedback forum, which has kept buyers and sellers honest for years, agents demonstrate a track record that's acceptable to the homeowner, and homeowners can exclude bids from agents who don't rank high enough.

This helps agents in obvious ways—you as the professional are able to compete for business that you don't even have to solicit! You respond to inquiries of already-interested parties. As your AgentRank™ increases, you're able bid on more listings that involve fewer agents. The consumer is also benefiting: An auction listing can be set up in less than ten minutes, and the system automates the realtor selection process by replacing interviews with the AgentRank™ system. Negotiations are replaced with auction-like bidding, and then within 48 hours, realtors and the seller can be introduced. Homeowners receive the realtor's profile, recent sales, and endorsements all online. If the seller is not happy with the agent, there is no obligation on the part of the seller.

Agents can sign up for no start-up fee, monthly fee, cancellation fee, or contract! Realtors should visit *www.realtybaron.com/agent* for information on signing up. Fees are paid only after a lead results in a closed sale.

This is yet another example of how an individual agent or real estate broker may "beat online competition" by partnering with organizations that are clearly ahead in the online real estate market.

We've talked about lots of technologies for the real estate professional, and partnering is one big way to really help improve your business position. So who else is out there for you to consider?

Take a look at Most Home Technologies Corporation, with documentation and product information available on their Web site at *www.mosthome.com*. Most Home has two products that you cannot miss before deciding what technology to implement.

Most Home became known for their ClientBuilder product line that builds on brokers' brands and proven lead response, qualification and incubation tools and services—leading to broker domination in many markets. Their system is Web-based, which is different from many others—and will also allow you to access it from anywhere. The system tracks leads—both sales and marketing—throughout the sales cycle. New associates get access through their broker and quickly set up full-featured Web sites, and they begin immediately benefiting from office-generated lead streams. This also proves a great retention tool or new-agent attraction tool for brokers; savvy real estate agents want to work for brokers with technology.

In 2005, Most Home acquired the assets of Executive Wireless. This gave Most Home the ability to create incredible products, including one that real estate professionals shouldn't miss! The product is called Executive Wireless, and it allows the transfer of detailed information from any database to any handheld device. Imagine, after reading through the chapter on technology, the possibilities here! Wireless Realty is their new flagship product and is a software application for handheld devices that will let you access critical industry and MLS data, that will eventually include ClientBuilder qualified leads. According to press releases, major organizations such as RE/MAX divisions are signing up with MostHome—yet another reason not to overlook their product. The team at MostHome understands that the way we market and generate sales in the Internet age is not the same way we used to, and they have created products to help you adapt and Web-enable your business. We already know the industry is moving toward integration, and this is a company that is well aware of it and positioning their solutions where you need them most.

REDESIGN YOUR OWN BUSINESS

This is really scary and difficult, and in many ways indicates a new career. While the fear factor is real, many in other service professions wish they had the heads-up that real estate professionals have. The complication of your industry has really given you an incredible advantage in being prepared for the pending changes. This may mean that you don't handle clients directly anymore, that you become an expert working for a larger company, or that you spend a considerable amount of your money investing in technology that makes you the middleman in an online transaction that still generates income. If you decide to stay in the industry, the traditional model may not work for you. If you choose to specialize as a first-time homebuying expert, holding the hands of frightened clients (certainly an option), working with boomers or investors, then begin marketing yourself that way now. Figure out what will help them, and start offering it. Think of the excitement of starting a new company, because that is essentially what you are doing.

This is both exciting and frightening at the same time. This scenario brings to mind a consultant to a real estate organization I worked for recently. He was outplaced by the consolidation of the telecommunications industry. While he held a professional sales position designing and selling enterprise network solutions to large companies, he found himself in a position in which his company merged with another, and he was quickly replaced by an individual who held the same position in the other company. Rather than trying to hunt and beg for new sales, he changed his career but used his expertise and relationships. He became a consultant for companies that needed help reviewing telecommunications contracts and network designs. As with many sales positions, the representatives for many of the telcos didn't always have their clients' best interests at heart. Not that they necessarily did damage, but they often padded solutions or costs and made suggestions that weren't in their clients' best interests.

This particular gentleman made a career out of helping companies review the proposals by telcos and then choosing the one that made the most sense. After doing so, he helped them make sure the network design wasn't overkill and that costs weren't built in that weren't necessary or were direct cost increasers. He got paid based on how much he saved the company, and even negotiated contracts on behalf of his client. He knew the business so incredibly well that he could read through the mumbo jumbo on the contracts and come to a solid and reputable conclusion, and he was (and is) well paid for his expertise. His years in the telco business weren't for naught, and he was able to develop a new career utilizing his partnerships and knowledge. Many of the companies he'd previously worked with as a salesperson became his clients as they negotiated new contracts and terms.

THE LEADER, THE EXPERT!

Have you considered the possibilities here? What if rather than having to push for listings and spending your weekends holding open houses, you were paid a fee to help review contracts your clients produced via the Internet? Or you searched the Internet lists for clients for a fee, and gave them lists of homes to show their buyer's agent—while, of course, working a partnership with the buyer's agent by which you get a referral fee? This would certainly reduce the scope of your job, but that isn't necessarily a bad thing depending on how you answered the first set of questions regarding what you like and dislike about your job the way it is.

First, this would require a partnership or referral setup (often with click-fees or kickbacks to the referring company, but it would be worth it) with the companies offering the online services. Next, you would need to establish yourself as a professional consultant, not only as an agent. Then, you'd work with your clients, who are obviously cost-conscious and saving money by listing their properties online and handling their transactions in cyberspace, to make sure contracts are structured properly and all the paperwork is in place. You'd charge a fraction of the traditional 5 percent to 6 percent and be considered an expert in your field.

If you're a mortgage broker, you may consider the same options but for the mortgage broker side. As already stated, I'd never recommend that anyone use a mortgage broker unless he or she has a special arrangement to avoid yield spreads, bogus fees, or hiked-up interest rates. If you are a mortgage broker and find yourself competing with direct-to-lender Web sites or even online brokers offering substantially lower rates, perhaps you should consider consulting for individuals to point out padded fees, potentially lower rates, or anything else you are intimately familiar with as an expert in your field. The value you would add in this new relationship far outweighs the value as a paper pusher while trying to scrape a margin off every transaction. Your perception in the industry would change rapidly as well.

Mortgage brokers are in another ballgame altogether. You are competing with negative publicity as well as the Internet. Mortgage brokers can become what the Internet mortgage Professor Uru Guttentag calls an upfront mortgage broker (UMB). These brokers disclose fees to customers in writing in advance and also disclose the wholesale prices that they are receiving from the lenders, credit customers with any rebates they receive from third parties, and many other things. This can be more thoroughly researched on Yahoo! Finance. This same author encourages individuals to shop for a mortgage online, as noted in several revisions of his articles. He indicates that shopping for a mortgage online is advised over traditional methods because online prices are easier to find and shop, pricing is often better, price volatility is easier to manage, consumers avoid "low-balling" pricing by lenders, and they avoid third-party settlement-cost low-balling. Consider putting your data online and even partnering with organizations that give more credibility to your line of work. On mtgprofessor.com, you can find a list of single-lender Web sites considered "worth shopping for" and a scoring system. Review these organizations and find out what makes them special, and then become so yourself.

WORK WITH INVESTORS?

What if you decided you'd rather spend your time analyzing markets, finding the next hottest area, and helping investors find rental property? You could be a one-stop shop—an assistant in finding a property manager, renters, locating the property, etc. This would utilize many of your existing skills yet expand them a bit, making you a relied-on expert and suddenly changing your business. You may still sell the homes for your investors at a discounted rate with some assurance they'd be back for their next purchase or sales transaction. The possibilities with a configuration such as this are endless but should be thought out if you enjoy this particular area of real estate. If you see yourself scoping out new markets, trying to find undervalued homes or areas, and helping your clients pull money from their existing properties to fund new investments, this may be a great area for you to consider and would align nicely with the future of real estate and the trend to view real estate as an investment. Beware though: This also requires partnerships with Web-based companies and a great degree of technology that positions you as an expert in particular markets or as an investment specialist. Successes here are all about the marketing and follow-through, so hiring an expert for Web-based marketing would be ideal and is recommended.

WORKING ON THE LEGAL SIDE

If you enjoy the legal side, consider working for a real estate attorney and providing advice to the attorney's clients—or even becoming an attorney. You would need to study a bit more about the laws associated with real estate transactions, but this is another great area of growth. As transactions become Web enabled, individuals will be turning to these attorneys for contract reviews and to help them seal electronic deals. There's a market here for your expanded expertise.

Consider offering your clients financial incentives to use your site over others. One popular referral site, ZipRealty.com, gives the client a kickback when a deal closes with one of their agents. Money talks and this company has done a great job capitalizing on this. It's also created partnerships with many organizations and receive click-through revenues for referrals. Consider new ways to make money by offering powerful space on your Web site. To do this, you need statistics and data on who is visiting your site and how often. This will help you sell your site as a viable market-ing tool for those working with you and buying advertising space on your site.

STAYING PUT

After careful consideration, you decide that you want to stay in business as you currently are, managing a traditional model and staying put in your world of real estate. That's okay, but you're going to have a more difficult time than if you choose otherwise. Most traditional real estate professionals are "jacks of all trades" but "masters of none." You will still find buyers for these services, such as first-time homebuyers or those less comfortable with tech-nology, but know that your market will be limited. You may need to begin working in an area that has more of the demographic you need, which would require a move and new research on your part. At the very least, prepare yourself for technology. Consumers aren't buying many of the old "tricks of the trade," so new tools need to be developed primarily for online customers. If your cus-tomer prefers the traditional methods, having the tools available certainly won't hurt and may even make your life easier. I don't recommend staying put—it isn't going to help you in a market-place that is all about expertise and niches.

EMBRACE FOR-SALE-BY-OWNER CLIENTS

A kind of hostility exists toward for-sale-by-owner sellers. I felt it personally when I decided to sell my primary residence myself, even though I was offering a commission to the agents who were representing the buyers. An agent who has tried his or her hard-est to get into a particular market and is a market expert in a spe-cific area sends flyer and calendar after notepad after magnet. Joe, after taking advantage of the block garage sales set up by the agent and using the notepads for grocery lists for years decides to sell his home, and he sells it by owner. This upsets you, and we understand why. But try to understand where your client is coming from. He or she may have paid only $200,000 for the house, so a 5 percent commission would have been $10,000. Now that house is worth half a million, and $25,000 is not chump change. Usually, those who sell by owner are doing so to avoid paying high fees and eating into profits, and the agent who has worked hard to solicit that business and indirectly build the relationship is not happy. Thus begins the friction between for-sale-by-owner clients and those selling through their local agent. The real estate agent feels robbed and taken advantage of, but the for-sale-by-owner seller never asked for those notepads to begin with! You must realize this because it's a key to embracing and not rejecting this growing segment of the market. Can you not represent buyers anyway? You will still earn the same commission if the seller is smart—2 percent to 3 percent—but your workload is far less. You certainly don't have to specialize in it; you don't even have to like it. But you do have to accept that it's a way of life for many of us. I have numerous partners in real estate, and I still sell myself unless I don't live in the area I am selling in (hint at yet another potential niche!).

For-sale-by-owner clients have come to realize that the fastest, most surefire way to sell their homes at reduced rates is to list on the Internet with MLS services. This means that for-sale-by-owner sellers have greater exposure than ever before in terms of finding buyers for their homes. MLS data are pulled from Realtor.com and the other top sites in the nation, as well as being accessible by real estate agents.

Sellers want to maximize visibility and real estate professionals should be thrilled—alas, they are not. Usually, the buyer will show you the property he or she is interested in; worst case, you will see it pop up as a new home for sale, and the seller, being more savvy today about selling by owner, will have noted the agent's percentage, or you can phone the seller to find out. You really have to do less work for the same amount of money. For-sale-by-owner sellers aren't as naive as one might think, nor are they as difficult to work with because of the tremendous amount of information that they have on the Internet available to them. They may even let you do the paperwork, which might decrease your stress of things potentially going wrong. In fact, this is yet another niche market—working with buyers who find homes on the Internet and sellers who pay less in commissions (perhaps the 1.5 percent to 2 percent rates).

Rather than fighting this trend, embrace those trying to save on the seller's fees. In reality, sellers' agents only get half anyway (maybe a half of 1 percent more if they are lucky), so they really shouldn't mind these individuals listing their homes on the MLS. Many others are still using traditional methods of advertising (yard signs and newspapers) and not listing their homes on the MLS or paying a buyer's agent fee. These homeowners haven't realized that buyers pay nothing to their agents to find homes, so they are really limiting their potential in the marketplace. As more and more people use tools online to sell, this need will become more apparent, and we'll see a greater percentage of for-sale-by-owner sellers paying buyers' agents' fees.

BUSINESS COMPETENCE

Studying your business and truly understanding the process in-depth is one way to help communicate your competence to potential clients. According to the National Association of Realtors®, people buy or sell homes approximately one time every six or seven years. This does not include investors, of course, but primary-residence homebuyers and homesellers. The real estate profession, laws, disclosure requirements, financing options, inventory, pricing models, and the market have changed as rapidly, or more so, in real estate than in other industries. Some buyers and sellers may want someone with this level of experience representing them, and this is one base of clients you want to capture. Doing so requires competence and experience that may not be replaced with online solutions.

BECOME AN AGENTS' AGENT

One option in the age of specialization is to market your business as a third-party, objective professional who provides advice to other agents looking for objectivity. Behind this idea is that the best lawyers don't represent themselves, the best doctors don't perform their own surgery, and the best real estate agents shouldn't represent themselves. You may charge a consulting fee to review contracts or provide services and market analysis to other agents who are representing themselves in transactions, which happens frequently. Some people even obtain real estate licenses just to get money back at the close of escrow! This is especially true in the investment markets where many individual investors have become licensed agents or brokers to collect their buyers' agents' fee. You may consider being a third-party objective agent to these brokers.

NEGOTIATIONS AND VALUATION EXPERT

You may choose to use your expertise in contract negotiations. Agents who are specialists in valuation, appraisals, and market conditions may choose to market themselves as negotiators for the best sales price (representing the buyer or the seller) and be there only for the negotiation of the deal. If you are good at negotiations, enjoy determining the value of homes, and like reading contracts, this might be a great niche to examine. You should consider this particularly if you have an aggressive personality and don't mind losing once in a while.

QUALIFY AND REFER

Another potential niche market is to focus on qualifying buyers and then passing them onto other agents for the home search. The agent who represents the buyer you qualified would pay you a portion of his or her commission for the qualification and lead. Your part in the transaction would be limited, and you would build rapport with the other real estate professionals, which does not have to exclude online organizations.

FOCUS ON SERVICE

By focusing on service, many travel agents have been able to maintain a loyal client base and even improve their sales in a largely Internet-driven market. Most have had to drop their price, and this is a reality of the situation. There is simply a greater supply of agents now, and as long as online sites continue to pop up, this will increase, putting yet more pressure on price. The process of "disintermediation" as many scholars call it (the removal of the middleman) may be overcome by focusing on service aspects of the business, such as using resources and referrals to their fullest. Buyers' agents may provide lenders, inspectors, individuals to fix up a home, or their own appraisers. This is a value-added service that Internet companies are trying to replicate but haven't quite succeeded at yet. Online organizations are looking for referral services so that the entire process, as in the Web-enabled scenario previously outlined, can be completed online. Focusing on ways in which you can add value from a service perspective may buy some time.

UNBUNDLE SERVICES

Unbundling previously packaged services, meaning that individuals could purchase any component of a professional's service that is of value to them, may guarantee some income in the future. This is true for real estate agents who may help a buyer find a home or a seller list on the MLS and create a virtual tour, but may not complete the entire sale for the full commission. Sales experts may offer lockbox services for a monthly fee, but not be there for open houses. The opposite may be true—perhaps you hold open houses for an for-sale-by-owner client, but you don't do any negotiation or paperwork. Some are adjusting their commission based on a pricing model designed to value the number and type of tasks they perform, working off a checklist by which the seller is ultimately in control and contracts with the agents for various tasks or advice. This is a component-based model that many other service industries have looked toward in the changing Internet economy. Mortgage brokers can use the same technique by perhaps helping an individual find a suitable loan with the list of lenders offering that type, or they may offer credit advice or income analysis while not completing the loan.

SPECIALIZE AND CONQUER

In the stock market, without trading on margin, an investor has to actually have the cash to buy the stock that then gains x percentage points in one year (we hope). Therefore, an investment of $15,000 at a 10 percent yearly rate of return nets about $1,500 in a year plus dividends, which are usually small. In real estate, however, $15,000 is a 10 percent down payment on a home that costs just shy of $150,000, including "prepaids" (taxes and insurance) and fees for the loan. This is where leveraging becomes essential.

Specializing in real estate investing may be one way to be considered a niche player and maintain or even improve your position despite the Web-based models. Analyzing a typical investor's way of thinking will help shed some light on this important topic.

Let's assume that the investment noted previously yields the same 10 percent return as the stock investment does. The stock appreciation or equity is 10 percent on the money invested. The real estate investment, however, is growing at 10 percent on the entire value of the home, not just on the down payment. Therefore, in one year the home is worth $165,000, an increase of $15,000—much better than $1,500! In most markets throughout the United States, real estate has appreciated faster than 10 percent per year and has appreciated far faster than the stock market when looking at it from a leveraging concept. Essentially in this example, the investor earned a 100 percent return on his or her invested money (the initial down payment of $15,000) in one year, not just 10 percent on the down payment. The individual investing in real estate is taking advantage of the concept of leveraging, letting the bank foot the bill for the remainder of the money that he or she will gain appreciation on. Renters pay the mortgage, and we sit back and watch our spreadsheets grow in net worth. There are, of course, the issues of collecting rent and making repairs, but this is where the property manager comes in. It's essential for investors to have good property management that minimizes the monthly deficit in rent and, in an ideal situation, at least breaks even on cash flow, thus creating zero liability for the investor but providing a nice return of 100 percent in a very conservative estimate. Banks rarely, if ever, do this for stock investors.

Taking this one step further, assume that the investor takes the equity of $165,000 minus the loan amount of $135,000 ($150,000 minus the down payment of $15,000) and pulls it out. This is $30,000 of equity, of which 90 percent is generally available through home equity lines of credit. Ninety percent of $30,000 is $27,000, enough to buy nearly two more properties. If the investor now puts in $3,000 of his or her money and buys two more properties, in one year, if the same holds true (and remember this is a conservative estimate!), the investor has $30,000 equity in two homes equaling $60,000, plus another $19,500 ($16,500 in appreciation plus the existing $3,000 not taken out the first time) on the first house, now totaling $79,500. Remember, the investor still only put in $18,000 of his or her money. In a two-year period, this is more than 400 percent in increases based on actual dollars invested—far better than any good year in the stock market. The real estate professionals that figure out the value of real estate and how to document it to those who invest have a bright future ahead with the right tools. The nation is no longer looking at real estate as just a "place to live," so why should real estate professionals? This is part of keeping up with the market.

Service-based companies aren't the only ones that have to specialize to survive. Even retailers who once enjoyed cushy margins and high profits are specializing just to stay in the game. Meredith Levinson in "A Season on the Brink," in the December 1, 2005, issue of *CIO* magazine, noted the increasingly popular online stores and declining sales in retail stores, specifically in nonspecialty stores. Does this sound familiar? Specialists are winning over the department stores that don't specialize in anything. The article notes that even "Santa" has abandoned department stores to move to the center of the mall, where shoppers are. Consumers spent $23.2 billion online during the 2004 Christmas season according to Goldman Sachs, Harris Interactive, and Nielsen//NetRatings, 25 percent over 2003. Holiday sales in stores in the same period from 2003 to 2004 rose only 2.3 percent, compared with 4 percent for 2002 to 2003. Two major department stores, JCPenney and Nordstrom, are the only ones seeing increasing sales and profit margins, and this is because of technology, according to their earnings spokespersons. These two organizations are embracing technology rather than fighting it; they've brought specialized merchandise into their stores, and as a result their numbers are soaring. On the other hand, those department stores still selling to the masses aren't faring so well, and the same trend is occurring in other online segments where specialization is key.

IT vendors have helped create customer-contact systems and ERP solutions that have changed these organizations' ability to provide what the customers really want, and this has revolutionized both their industry and their sales. Competition is not happy, and your competition could feel the same way if you adequately embrace technology. Nordstrom, for example, has applied its traditional customer-contact books to a modern customer relationship management (CRM) application, something agents can do on a smaller scale. Inventory management is also huge in these retail industries, and similar technologies such as managing homes for sale and lease are essential to agents and other real estate professionals. This is one example of how technology is changing industries and those with specialized knowledge are making their way into the new era.

WHAT IF I'M AN APARTMENT MANAGER, PROPERTY MANAGER, OR LEASING AGENT?

A sector of the market ignored too often in books like this is the apartment leasing community and the professionals who work in this business. This includes apartment and property managers and leasing agents. While real estate agents have lots of resources available to them, those who work in the apartment industry often find themselves buried in an Internet-savvy market with little help. Yet, we know that to become or remain technically savvy and to create sales in a market that is often Internet-based, you need to have services available to clients that will aid them in their selection process and truly provide the ease of use that many individuals are looking for. Multifamily rental housing is often an attractive investment opportunity for individuals and large institutional investors. The average return for investors from 1984 to 2004 was 9.3 percent, compared with 7.6 percent for all other property types. No wonder this is such a hot market! Before we get into the specifics about a site you cannot miss if you are in this market sector, let's take a look at some demographics.

So just who is renting? As of 2004, according to the Census Bureau, 24.9 percent of housing in the United States had at least two units and were considered apartments. Within these homes lived 11 percent of married couples, 27.4 percent of individuals where the man was living alone, 32 percent of individuals where the female is living alone, and 50.7 percent of singles. A full 32.9 percent of potential living quarters in the United States is occupied with renters, including single-family residences and apartments. This represents nearly half of all single individuals, and roughly 17 percent of all married couples (U.S. Census Bureau,

2004). This is an incredible market with a demographic that often looks online for their next home.

Demographics for users appear to vary by site. In the late 1990s, Rent.net published their statistics showing that their average renter was between 23 and 26 years old, with the mean falling between 20 and 35 years old. Generally the users were college graduates preparing to move to a new city for a new job. Yet, at the time, AllApartment.com published demographics indicating that their range was between 18 and 55 years old; indicating to some that the Internet was gaining momentum in the older population of individuals (Realty Times). Sites that were only recently unheard of (such as Craig's List) have become so popular to find apartments on that *The Wall Street Journal* noted in 2002 that Craigslist was making a "dent" in the New York area apartment market (Saranow, 2002).

So who is living in apartments today? The National Multi Housing Council has published data from 2003 that appear to be the latest we have on this topic, but most believe the numbers haven't changed much. The data are different than you might suspect! Apartment renters are most likely to be between the ages of 30 to 64, representing a full 66 percent of the market; 20 percent are 65 or more years old, and just 13 percent are under the age of 30. The median age for apartment renters is 47 years. Specific to apartments, renters are most likely to be a husband/wife/kid(s) family at 26 percent, with a husband with wife only falling in a close second at 21 percent. Single females make up 15 percent of the group and single males 12 percent. "Other," unidentified in the study, makes up a relevant 17 percent of total apartment renters. Households who rent having two members make up 33 percent of the market; 27 percent have just one member. Households with four or more people make up 24 percent of the market, with the mean being 2.5 persons. The mean number of children under the age of 18 that adults have living in their apartment homes is six, representing 32 percent apartment renters that have at least one child living in the home. In addition, 23 percent of apartment renters make less than $20,000; 20 percent make between $20,000 and $34,999; 15 percent make between $36,000 and $49,999; 17 percent make between $50,000 and $74,999; and a surprising 25 percent make over $75,000 per year! Plus, 90 percent are non-Hispanics, and 10 percent are Hispanics. The average apartment renter has 1.8 cars, and 91 percent of them have more than one car. The state with the highest number of individuals renting apartments is the District of Columbia at 35 percent, followed by New York at 23 percent (NHMC, 2003).

We already know that print advertising for homes and apartments is down. We know more and more people, particularly the groups that are within the demographic represented for apartments, are using the Internet at steadily increasing rates to find data or information that they want, instantaneously—about 12 million of them monthly (IDXDirect). This incredibly savvy client requires that you, the professional, be even savvier. There is one organization you should become intimately familiar with if you are responsible or have influence over an organization that leases or rents apartments.

VaultWare has a site at *www.vaultware.com* that makes it easier to lease out apartments. The solution, in conjunction with Realty DataTrust (a known credible expert in online leasing), curious shoppers can become serious prospects. Take a look at their site and pay close attention to the capability added, such as providing access to current apartment availability, rents, amenities, and specials. Prospects can reserve and prescreen specific apartments without even contacting you by phone! VaultWare is a reservation system in the apartment industry that you need to be familiar with. It will bring you, as an apartment leasing agent, a real prospect that is committed to the leasing process.

One major benefit to using VaultWare is that the system helps eliminate a lot of calls and questions that are about logistics, availability, and price and allows the leasing agent to see a pop-up when someone is truly interested in a property. This is important because more time can be spent doing business and less time can be spent just answering questions from casual lookers or individuals who are not genuine prospects. VaultWare is partnered with numerous organizations you are already familiar with and trust; they provide a complete list of these partners at *www.vaultware .com/partners/*.

Another recently launched product is a newsletter called the *Apartment Internet Marketing Newsletter*, or AIM. As of May 2006, the second newsletter had appeared online. This is a great resource for all sorts of information apartment-related, including technology and its impact on the market. The founder of Vault-Ware has produced this great newsletter and you can access it online at *apartmentinternetmarketing.com/newsletter/aimissue2.html*. The newsletter also features video on "top technology icons" and other relevant topics.

The Internet has created a marketplace in all areas of real estate where a person who wants to move to a new city doesn't even need to visit the city before moving; with integrated maps, demographic data, and the ability to find places to live (including apartments), the need to put such information on the Internet and become affiliated with or partnered with these types of organizations is growing infinitely.

EMBRACE NEW TECHNOLOGIES

A slew of new technologies are out there that you may or may not be welcoming into your business. It's important that you do so because you will be a more attractive buyer's or seller's agent to those who are interested in doing business at least in part via the Internet.

One of the essential portions of this book is to review these new technologies and help you understand and embrace them. Some of the most critical ones today are given here:

- Instant messaging (IM) allows you to send immediate, quick messages to your clients or partners using your computer. Two of the most popular IM clients are Microsoft's Messenger and AOL's Instant Messenger. If you want to appeal to a larger crowd, install a piece of software that connects to both systems (like Trillian) and offer up both IM addresses on your business cards. You'll be amazed how many people can't make phone calls from their cubicles at work but can IM you with questions or updates that go unnoticed by their bosses or colleagues.

- Another option is to use a lead-based text-messaging system. The reason this is so important is that many consumers who are searching for an agent want immediate responses and don't want to wait for calls a day or two down the road—or even an hour. Companies such as QWASI Inc. created CellSigns that lets buyers get information on properties via messaging and sends instant messenger leads to agents. In fact, this is entirely cell-phone capable, and buyers can receive information directly on their text-enabled cell phones.

- Which brings us to another technology—cell phone text messaging. Several of the agents I work with explicitly ask their callers in their outgoing voice mail message to *not* leave a text message. This is completely incomprehensible! Let them leave a text message! In fact, *respond to them by text message!* If they messaged you that way it's because they want to be communicating with you in this manner. It's easy to use and cheap.

- WiFi access—and I don't just mean at hotspots. With the ability today to use wireless access PCMCIA cards in your laptop, there is no reason to not have full connectivity. When you are at an open house, you can easily respond to clients, leaving those browsing around the home feeling that they have freedom to look around. This access makes you more productive and keeps you responding quickly on weekends when more families may be prone to searching for homes and sending e-mails to agents. Check out Verizon's newest Wireless Anywhere product, which is far more convenient than hotspots, though not quite so fast. All the major cell providers have this capability as well, so check around.

- Pay to have your site rank higher in Web site searches. After you've determined what your specialty will be, your Web site creator should use meta tags (tags to identify the content on your Web page) that Web search agents will use to find your site. You can pay to have your site, based on particular criteria, escalated in the search results. As Web traffic and Web-initiated sales grow, this will be a worthwhile investment.

- Invest in a good-quality digital camera. Sometimes buyers will ask for pictures beyond what is listed in the MLS. Investing in a good digital camera and good editing software to crop and brighten up pictures is an essential must-have, as is the laptop to send them on.

- Electronic forms. There are numerous systems out there today providing the paperless office to real estate agents. Do some searching and talking to those who are successfully using one, and make the switch. You will be pleasantly surprised—and your clients will be thrilled.

- A portable printer. As odd as this may sound, it is an essential tool. Let's say you are sitting at an open house and someone wants to make an offer. Having the ability to print there without lugging around heavy equipment will be a lifesaver, guaranteed. Both Canon and HP make very good printers for under $250. Not to mention a sense of urgency can be created on the spot; but tools are needed to do so.

- Electronic mail-marketing software is also essential. This allows you to customize your marketing campaign to leads that you have received, provides you with electronic news-letters (with some packages), and lets you manage who gets what data and when.

- Create electronic-mail templates for various correspondences. This will show you are truly Web enabled and that you are going the extra mile to work by e-mail. Some of the templates you may wish to create (and then fill in times, names, etc.) are appointments, what to bring to document signings, and utilities to call to turn on service in certain areas. You can spruce them up with relatively inexpensive ($30 or less) software from Download.com, and you can customize e-mail as well. Be sure to check on the reliability and validity of the software before downloading, or buy a major package from your local office supply store for under $50 and avoid the risk of having Spyware installed on your PC.

- Embrace online faxing tools to replace the paper fax machine. Standard contracts and documents can be edited in Word or PDF editing software and then sent via software like My Fax (*www.myfax.com*) or eFax (*www.efax.com*). They provide electronic confirmations of sent faxes and also let you manage incoming faxes. You can receive all faxes in your e-mail in-box and have one less thing to check. Plus, traveling to those open houses is far easier if you have the ability to print faxes from wherever you are without having to go to the office.

- Get your own domain name! It's relatively easy and inexpensive to register your own domain name, for instance, *sally@sallysrealty.com*. This gives the consumer confidence that you have embraced technology and gives the appearance of a large shop. Companies such NameSecure (*www.namesecure.com*) and many other competing organizations offer the ability to register your site, host it with them for flat-out cheap rates, and host your e-mail accounts that can manage exceptionally sized attachments. Do shop around and get the best deal.

- Lose the Web-based e-mail system. The power of a system that lets you create folders and easily view data, create rules to be run automatically, and create professional-looking signatures while connecting to multiple in-boxes is highly understated in today's efforts to be technologically savvy. Lose the Web-based e-mail system and go for a POP3 compatible client, like Microsoft Outlook, Outlook Express, or many of the others that are common today. CNET.com offers a great review of various e-mail clients.

- Use antispam software religiously to keep from being bogged down with unsolicited and virus-causing, spyware-enabling e-mail. Server-side software can keep you from ever having to see the mail but runs the risk of trashing something that wasn't really spam mail. Client-side software usually puts the mail into a folder, creating the need to rummage through it anyway. Choose the one that best fits your goals.
- Don't force potential customers to use forms on your Web site. Offer a plain old e-mail address *and* a form, and let them choose. While you're at it, forget the autoresponders that say, "Sally is out of the office but will get to your message soon." That sends the *wrong* message. Instead, get consistent access to the Internet and respond with a real message. Autoresponders are nothing short of annoying to those who receive the messages.
- Use a personal digital assistant, or PDA, preferably one that is connected to the Internet live. This will help you manage appointments; store contacts; and, if you are connected to the Internet, look up information, maps, and directions, or e-mail clients from anywhere. Some like the Treo provide enhanced services including cellular phone access so you only need one device. Sony also makes a PDA that uses a memory stick that's also used in its digital cameras and some MP3 players, making it rather convenient and portable. Some MLS download systems and lockbox software requires a Palm device, so check with your providers before making the decision.
- Get your own demographic systems that are robust and better than what your consumers can get online. Consider products like Maptitude from Caliper, which you can research and try out at *www.caliper.com*.
- Create a great storage system online. This goes back to the e-mail folders. If you have everything stored in a folder in an e-mail to yourself, you can simply forward the e-mail to your client. Contracts? Paperwork? Just forward an e-mail al-

ready stored and typed out. Talk about less hassle! Your client will appreciate the immediate response, too.

- Don't spam your customers or prospects. Offer them a way to disengage from your mailing lists, and don't wait the "ten days" some sites offer to do it. Sending unsolicited mail or mail that just isn't wanted anymore is a surefire way to upset a lot of people and even get your e-mail address or worse yet, your domain, blocked by some Internet service providers (ISPs). Offer an opt-in, but also offer an opt-out. Don't put someone on your e-mail mailing list unless he or she actually asks to be on it or if he or she selects "Yes" on a box on a form online.

- Get a GPS. Not only will this save you time when you're looking at homes that are for sale, your clients will appreciate it when you go to look at houses. Face it, you can't know every street in every city your buyers may want to look.

- Use virus protection and antispyware tools. Two great antispyware tools are Ad-Aware and SpyBot Search and Destroy. These will help ensure your computer stays running smoothly, and the antivirus software will not only protect your data, it will help ensure you don't transmit viruses to your clients—surefire ways to have them dislike you.

- Use backup software, whether it's online or a DVD. For only a few dollars a month, you can use tools that back up your hard drive online to another off-site storage site. If you don't want to shell out the cash or want a copy somewhere else, use DVDs or another external hard drive that you can store in a *different* place than your computer in case of natural disaster. You can get backup software at your local computer or office supply store or off the Internet. Some great free tools are even available at Download.com, but beware of spyware hidden in the code.

You may not be able to embrace a full paperless office right now, or you may not be able to afford to partner with a company offering complete transactions online in the future, but at the very least offer electronic forms and forget the habits of the past. CDM Inc. offers numerous products to help agents obtain electronic signatures, real estate forms, and transaction-management systems. While the industry hasn't fully embraced digital signatures, it's certainly well on its way, and you need to be at the top of the movement.

The same company mentioned previously also offers solutions for buyers to "sign" documents remotely using a power of attorney and automates the closing process for lenders and buyers. Closing Stream is one such package and worth looking into. About 15 percent of closing packages are returned because of an error in the notary or processing, and it can take three to four days to send out paperwork overnight and get it processed. Software like this can streamline this process into hours.

In 1999, the Real Estate Transaction Standard was adopted and supported by the National Association of Realtors® as the standard in information systems. As this continues to demand more from agents and other real estate professionals, the move to the paperless office continues driving forward.

If you are a mortgage broker, bank, or other lender, consider software such as Online Documents' eMortgageDocs, which supports paperless mortgage processes. Online Documents even developed an eHud software solution to make sure any changes made by agents are reflected in closing documents. Initial disclosures are also sent to applicants using a "click to accept" method online. Many believe the mortgage business will be the driving force behind the push to paperless transactions due to the perception of cost savings. Even online notary services are available with electronic signatures coming from a Palm PDA device.

Some additional ways to make technology work for you include:

- Get a "follow-me" telephone number, the kind that will first ring your office, then your cell, and then your pager (in whatever order you like). This single number can be used anywhere and will give your clients the ability to contact you without having to phone several different numbers. While you are at it, consolidate e-mails so that any e-mail addresses are accessible from anywhere and they all come into one e-mail in-box that you can organize.

- Embrace the idea of unified messaging (UM). Many Voice over IP (VoIP) carriers and even some free stand-alones (like K7.net) offer services that allow callers to send voice mail right into your e-mail in-box. This can be incredibly useful and convenient, allowing you to store the associated files in the folder of your favorite e-mail client.

- Consider the use of VoIP in your business. It offers many advantages, including the ability to call other areas with no additional cost or surf the Web from your Internet-enabled phone, depending on the features of your system. Best of all, these systems often include unified messaging features built right in. VoIP really sells itself if you are running a company with multiple offices. With it, all the offices are on extension dialing and long-distance costs in those areas are a thing of the past. Complex VoIP systems from companies such as Cisco or Avaya replace entire existing phone infrastructures and require configuration and setup, but their return on investment is often at a break-even point quickly, particularly if your offices are in cities that have cheap Internet access. If you have a single or home office, however, consider companies like Skype or Vonage, both of which will also support using Web cameras so you can see and hear your clients. Clearly, this is partly a cost-savings mechanism and not only a technological competitive advantage.

- Invest in a good solid PDF generator. No doubt, you are already using these in your business; a good PDF generator and editor will let you edit PDFs, allow your clients to sign them and return them to you, and convert them into other application formats like Word or Excel, and vice versa.

- Get rid of your desktop and replace it with a portable laptop that has an excellent screen; or better yet have both. You can use this in open houses or at a remote office, especially if you work out of your home. Coupled with WiFi Anywhere mentioned earlier, you have a truly remote and portable office with incredible power and capability unthinkable just a few years ago.

- Invest in a good cell phone camera that will allow you to download contacts to your desktop computer. This is, of course, if you decide against the PDA/phone combo route. A camera phone will let you instantly take pictures of properties your clients might like; find one with good resolution, at least one megabyte. Samsung makes an excellent camera phone with good resolution and flash. You can instantly send these via text messaging or picture mail or by e-mail to your clients.

SUMMARY

In this chapter, we've brainstormed and explored many of the things you can do today to stay current and the things you can do to prepare yourself for tomorrow's technology. Take these considerations to heart, but only implement those that fit with your character, your personality, and what you love to do. When you love your work, it will show. Enthusiasm is contagious, and you want to be as enthusiastic about what you do as you can be. Most of these recommendations will either streamline your business or save you money and will embrace your most technically savvy clients and those not afraid to do some of the work themselves. These markets need not escape you as a real estate professional, but you must take the time to prepare yourself to work with these people. Remember, they are smart, computer-literate, and Internet savvy—and have very high expectations. Also remember—this crowd tends to not succumb to the methods that real estate professionals have been using for marketing and they want to shop around for the absolute best price. Human contact isn't always required; an e-mail address will do just fine.

7

INVESTORS CREATING MARKETS RIPE FOR THE PICKING

According to 2004 Fannie Mae economic data, many investors have resorted to real estate as a replacement for stocks and bonds that they haven't been satisfied with. In certain, more extreme cases, individuals have funneled some of their retirement income into rental properties. Some areas show a 30 percent or more investor saturation, thus leading into the discussion in this chapter—the making of markets. We already discussed this a bit with regard to what you need to do as a real estate professional to accommodate those who look to real estate as an investment and not only as a primary home purchase. This discussion is important because one of the best ways to survive the coming technological changes will be to focus on investors. You can't do that without understanding the role the Internet is playing in the making of markets. You need to understand several aspects of investors and what homeowners think so that you don't offend people who are potential clients in the midst of capturing new markets.

HOMEOWNER OPINIONS

Homeowners in various areas have a love-hate relationship with investors. You must consider this if you decide to work almost exclusively or exclusively with investors. To give you a personal example: I recently returned from a trip to Austin, Texas, where I own rental property. I talked with more than 20 people while visiting, not telling them immediately why I was there (as I am often asked as a first question on striking up a conversation), and I quickly turned the conversation to their real estate market, their economy, and how they feel about the booming investor market.

Interestingly enough, homeowners and residents didn't feel nearly as bullish about their market as I (and my investor-colleagues and friends) feel about particular areas of the undervalued Austin, or at least the perception of it. I had to think: Did they just not do their homework? Were they not as smart as my friends? Did they not see what was happening in their own neighborhoods? Then, after asking more questions, I realized that they, in general, didn't like us (in fact, their mood changed quickly when I finally answered the "So why are you here?" question with "I'm looking at my investment property that I purchased with only digital pictures and electronic signatures," and if it weren't for the design center of a particular homebuilder requiring my on-site visit, I probably never would have gone. I usually left that part out.). The truth is I saw something in their backyards that they didn't. I was given information from human resources and then did my own research online, verifying what looked like a buyer's market.

Perhaps it is a lack of information, but they aren't happy that we're raising their prices and creating too many rental properties. Do you think they will be happy that you are helping us? Probably not. So you need to be prepared for this and accept it, or learn to find ways to show these homeowners the benefits investors are enjoying in their areas—and there are many. We aren't really creating these markets; they already exist. They used to be owned and run by locals; now, however, they're often owned by people living in other states and managed by locals. Residents aren't happy their homes are considered undervalued and they certainly want to maintain what they call a standard of living that includes a small town feel and lots of open land. In some areas, there was a strong resistance to building period, whether that meant a freeway on-ramp, a mall, or a house. You may have spent a long time building a reputation in these areas as homeowner-friendly, and you don't want to damage it too badly in case the investor market fails.

As demand increases, homeowners' opinion of their lifestyle moves in the opposite direction. Shopping malls? New freeways? Not for us: "Keep it in California" I heard about half a dozen times in three days. Yet, the builders seemed to have a different viewpoint. Driving down the major highways, I saw numerous signs for builders offering huge homes (by California standards) for under $180,000, another amazing tale of the fortunes available as perceived by those in highly priced markets. That $180,000 wouldn't buy my 5,000-square-foot backyard in California. This is yet another option for you in real estate—many times major homebuilders offer commissions to agents who bring buyers to their new home communities. You may choose to partner with some of them and keep homeowners happy while still making good commissions from companies that don't mind paying for them.

Why is this critical to this book? Simple—the Internet has been one of the primary catalysts for the huge increase in investment purchases throughout the United States. I am using Austin, Texas, as an example because it's the one I am currently most familiar with, though you can bet others will be added to the mix soon—almost all of them located by investment companies that use the Internet to do research or my own primary Internet-based research. You don't want to alienate your primary market while you begin to create your new niche.

On this trip, I took time particularly to informally interview individuals about their opinions on investors, investments, and their general outlook on their economy. I had one individual, a flight attendant flying to Dallas who was off-duty, tell me I made a "huge mistake" moving into one particular area of northern Austin, Round Rock, because "he's lived there for three years and it isn't all that great." "All that great" doesn't necessarily define a bad investment. My data show otherwise. My data, from the Internet, indicate that much like other areas in Arizona and Nevada over the past couple of years, Texas will soon be the new booming area and I'm not the only one with this opinion. In fact, at a recent motivational seminar in Los Angeles, several speakers who were representing real estate companies specifically mentioned the Texas market and Austin in particular.

WORK TO CREATE MARKETS!

This Internet-savvy group of individuals is using Web tools to literally make markets. In a future book, a colleague and I will explore the making of markets by investors in greater detail. For now and to keep on topic, I'll discuss the use of the Internet in this phenomenon labeled by Dr. Lazo and myself as "marketing making." Investors are consistently turning to the Internet to gain viable insight and information on potential new markets and to explore availability and expected gains. Internet tools for many create a sense of understanding, insight, and stability not experienced by previous investors. You can be a part of the market making of areas if you can partner with companies who find them first—or do it yourself like the investors do.

INVESTORS BETTING ON TANGIBLE PROPERTY

According to *Bloomberg News* in April 2005 in "Investors Bet on New Homes," 9 percent of all home sales in 2004 in the United States were made by investors. Nearly one in ten home sales had nothing to do with making a life for oneself in a new home (unless you count early retirement), but rather using real property to make money. Other statistics show this as high as 25 percent of all purchases made in 2004 and 2005. If you were reinventing your business, would you not want to potentially tap into this market?

Everyone needs a place to live and investors know that. The economy-stifling decisions made by the federal government (I know many of you will disagree) recently have given stocks a bad reputation for increasing or decreasing in value for seemingly ridiculous or speculative reasons with no logic behind it, while real estate is perceived by many of us to be the stable investment and to nearly guarantee appreciation over time; provided you have enough cash flow, it's a no-brainer. Work with these investors and as that section of the market increases you are sure to not only hang onto commissions but perhaps upsell other services in the process.

Two of the keys for investors are having enough cash flow from the properties that as an investor, you can hang in there through the rough times (if there is, in fact, a downturn, which I will blame almost entirely on the federal government and its worry over inflation based on a new market that the older people who are running it don't understand) and locked-in interest rates for the foreseeable future (three to five years, even seven in some cases) to keep the payment locked. Understand what impacts us most, and we will be even more likely to want to work with you. I have found that those who know investing tend to stick together—a real estate agent in the Austin market who I did not know happened to know my property manager, not because Austin is a small city but because they both deal with investors. Networking in this community is not a bad thing.

FINDING THE NEXT HOT MARKET—THE TECHNOLOGY WAY

As a California investor, I'd never invest in the California or Nevada overinflated markets; I need, therefore, to find my next location and information about those areas online. In many cases, buyers can go online and even find homebuilders willing to sell to investors directly, fax in some paperwork, and five months later have a house that's already appreciated more than a really good stock portfolio will in three years. It is so easy that it seems ludicrous not to invest. When I talk with people not doing it and I ask them why, almost invariably the answer is one of two responses: either they don't know where to start or they are afraid and generally not interested in taking risks. Education, in particular by real estate professionals who become experts in these areas, can help mitigate both of those issues and create inherent demand and business for themselves. Remember that these risk-averse people are those who actually order a stock certificate because they don't trust online trading companies to keep records! I haven't discounted them entirely from the future market because with enough education, hopefully they also will be able to see the value in this great investment potential.

First, we research locations that are undervalued or have just begun a rapid increase in price. Then after narrowing it down to about five or so locations, we do intense demographic research, looking for telltale signs of an increase in demand (such as a large company moving to the city) or alternatively a decrease in demand (such as a military base closing). After narrowing it down, we research business journals and newspapers to find out what is happening in the various cities, and then we have a city to work with. We find properties using sites such as ZipRealty or REALTOR.com, and then we make our deals. This is where you could fit in, whether you are a lender, a mortgage broker, a real estate agent, or an appraiser. Some have even created new businesses through which they work for investors to "investigate" properties before they are bought—one step beyond that of an inspector to tell us what a house is *really* like. In some investor-hot markets, 80 percent or more of the purchases and sales are by investors; homeowners in those areas are often taking advantage of the increase in price and leaving the area while capitalizing on far greater than expected returns (or would have otherwise occurred without the Internet and the investors). This is at the heart of the love-hate relationships smaller towns have with investors. Perhaps if you find an area where investors are moving in, you'll also find homeowners wanting to move out—a market ripe for the picking.

For investors, I've noted two major schools of thought: Buy in the areas that appear undervalued and wait for them to appreciate before moving into yet another undervalued market, or buy in areas already developed that have infrastructure with no "waiting" involved. Both methods involve some risk, and others take the position of balancing their portfolios with both types of investments. Regardless, often the property agent (if one is used) and property-management company are found using Internet search engines.

FINDING MARKETS TO SELL IN—FIRST!

Let's look at an example or two of how the Internet helps create markets, and then look at the potential role the real estate agent plays in this new marketplace. We'll also look at how the investor or homebuyer can benefit by these changes and create a win-win situation for the real estate professional and the homeowner or investor.

Take, for example, the two cities of Bullhead City, Arizona, and Round Rock, Texas. In the case of Bullhead City, investors knew about the possible boom even before homebuilders caught on, something that we're seeing more today with the Internet than ever before. In the "old days" (more than five years ago in real estate investing), many people would follow the major builders (or Home Depot) when predicting which areas would have sustainable appreciation. Now investors are looking to be one step ahead of the builders, getting in supercheap and letting the property appreciate. Many fundamentals must be looked at as well, for instance, the rate of unemployment in the area or the average income as well as rental comparative analyses. These data are also available on the Internet.

Back to Bullhead City. Who has heard of this city anyway? Unless you are a frequent visitor to Laughlin or Lake Havasu, you've probably not familiar with it and you may still not be. I began working with an investment company a couple of years ago that insisted I buy property out there. I bought two lots and a single-family residence. The two lots cost $35,000 and $20,000, and the single-family residence (three bedrooms and two baths) cost $120,000. With regard to the SFR, for a mere $12,000 investment (10 percent down), within two years I had a bank appraisal (without even having to do an on-site, which traditionally come in low) of $180,000, generating nearly $54,000 in capital to reinvest in other properties without selling the home, all while enjoying positive cash flow on a home that has had exactly four weeks without rent. Not a bad deal. This particular real estate agent, top in his knowledge of investor markets, has made a fortune helping investors find the next hot market, setting up a one-stop shop including property management, and then calling investors he knows have equity positions to convince them to buy. He's trusted for his instincts and his intense negotiation skills, among other things.

So how did I find out about Bullhead City? Well, the investment partner I work with provided preliminary information. The Internet was the primary source of data and the basis for determining that this was a highly undervalued market. Since then, I have conducted my own research, but everyone needs to get started somewhere. You could create a company that helps investors find markets and then help them build wealth. Who doesn't need someone to help them do that? It is a full-time job to find properties and make deals. With the investment company buying almost the entire inventory within a couple of months because it trusted its data and its instincts, demand increased (other investors followed) and supply was near zero, with new homes coming on the market at incredibly increased prices. Amazingly enough, it was only after this all began we saw the homebuilders move in! Essentially between the Internet and the investors, a new market was made and it has sustained its value while continually appreciating at an above-average rate.

What about Round Rock, Texas? It's in a similar situation, although the homebuilders were there before most investors in this particular case. Round Rock sits outside of Austin in Texas and is a higher-end community with significant new infrastructure that will accommodate a larger population and tremendous industry growth. While there is still a lot of open land to build on, once the land quantity diminishes, the supply will decrease while demand is increasing thanks in part to the Internet but mostly because of the investors. There is another lesson to be learned from all of this. The homebuilding industry does a lot of research in marketing; I worked for one for years as a technology director. We knew that when clients asked us to e-mail them, they meant it. We knew that when they said they didn't want to be contacted about anything until the home was done and someone local could "pick the options," they meant it. We didn't try to hold their hand; we figured out who was savvy and who wasn't. This really appealed to buyers who were buying second homes or investment properties or were just hands-off kind of people. Real estate professionals can learn a valuable lesson from this marketing fact.

HOW REAL ESTATE PROFESSIONALS CAN CAPITALIZE ON INVESTORS

Successfully navigating the Internet era in real estate will require real focus and dedication on the part of the real estate professional. One way real estate professionals, whether on the lending, property management, or sales agent side, can capitalize on these changes is by understanding and embracing the investor market. By becoming familiar with the nuances and demands of investors, agents and other professionals can choose this as their specialty when it comes to their new marketing efforts. This may require subscription to multiple MLSs or becoming an area expert from a new perspective—from that of an investor. You may find yourself having to become familiar with what a three-bedroom SFR in "area 10" rents for and what areas have the highest rental demand while enjoying the lowest unemployment rates, or you may find yourself studying rules, benefits, and risks with Section

8 housing. Regardless of which area of specialty you choose, if it involves dealing with investors there's a great deal to learn.

Remember that being an investors' agent requires an intense knowledge of the area you are representing and working in. We have already noted that one way for you to be a successful agent in today's fiercely competitive market is to be a specialist. eNeighborhoods provides a solution for you to do this while integrating your current important data sets and Web presence. What makes this solution a competitive advantage is its incredible power and answer-driven model, as you'll see in this section of the book. If you want to *beat* the online competition, you need to offer more than the Web alone can offer. This package addresses potential questions and issues that would take hours of searching with less than stellar results.

There are a lot of technology companies out there trying to help you, the professional realtor or broker, survive and flourish in a technology-enabled world. There are a small handful of those companies that truly understand what you need and what your clients want—and one that cannot be missed is eNeighborhoods. Long before putting this book together, I was looking at their technology and the incredible power it has created for real estate professionals.

Most studies show that the neighborhood a person moves into is the most important deciding factor in their purchase decision. This is especially true for individuals who intend to live in the home they are buying. Many of you have made a living being a neighborhood or area expert, only to have technology replace much of your hold on the marketplace. With map overlays, the ability to look online for demographics and school information, some realtors have not capitalized on their knowledge of areas as a competitive advantage. Along comes eNeighborhoods to give you credibility, data, and a professional image.

The Neighborhood Report is a compilation of data that eNeighborhoods has been collecting on just about every neighborhood aspect you could imagine. Crime, schools, statistics on individuals with children in the area—if your client can think to ask it, eNeighborhoods can answer. The system not only addresses questions such as these with its incredible data bank, but it also prints and generates incredible reports that are easy for your client to interpret and use to make a decision. Imagine being able to provide your client with information like this: the average SAT score is for the area, the student-teacher ratios, and the number of National Merit finalists?! Yes your clients can get data online, but this is far better than they will get unless conducting thorough, extremely time-consuming searches. Herein lies the competitive advantage! Yes it is true that all of these data are available on the Internet, but the incredible amount of time it would take to sort through it and create true information from the raw data would take you so long that the return on investment may not be there. With this product, it's sure to be.

In addition to the incredible data-driven information you can give your clients, they can see a birds-eye view of their potential purchase. In partnership with GlobeXplorer, a leading provider of satellite images and aerial photography, you can give your clients a sense of the neighborhood they are considering a move into. eNeighborhoods uses block-level data, not zip code–level data, which provide greater accuracy and more information on demographics. You can get a comprehensive look at any neighborhood by blending the MLS data, the BuyerTour, and the Neighborhoods Report data for an incredibly powerful tool.

One area taking off for this organization is providing MLSs with access software. In about 70 mainly large MLS systems, the majority of the agents in the area use their eNeighborhoods Wyldfyre product for daily access to their MLS, as the MLS has licensed their product for the membership. This access software lets agents pull the data into their PC and create professional reports that made eNeighborhoods famous—including blending MLS data with proprietary neighborhood information, maps, aerials, etc. MLSs around the country are now buying their products for membership and they are being recognized as the industry standard.

Above and beyond all these tools, eNeighborhoods allows you to integrate the neighborhood data into your own broker or MLS sites. This is an alternative to the XML system we've discussed earlier. To add to their credibility, eNeighborhoods hosts *www.HelpUSell.com* and was selected as a RE/MAX technology partner. In fact, they are so highly regarded, RE/MAX selected them to create an entire backbone for their franchise network. eNeighborhoods aggregated the MLS listing data that appears on the network and created a lead management system called Lead-Street, which is accessible to 100,000+ associates through their intranet, MainStreet. All leads captured off RE/MAX.com get incubated in LeadStreet, where all the eNeighborhoods tools are integrated in a customized RE/MAX platform. This system is capturing thousands of leads per day; prior to this, only RE/MAX listings were accessible to consumers. Talk about amazing capability and a strong organization! RE/MAX was the first national real estate organization, thanks to these efforts, to give consumers access to all listings anywhere in the United States at their Web site *www.remax.com*. This has every home for sale featured, regardless of which company holds the listing. The system requires no referral fees or registration.

In 2005, Deloitte ranked it on the Technology Fast 500, and it's an endorsed benefit partner of NAR. To top that, they were selected number 84 on the Inc. 500 list. For more information, visit *www.eneighborhoods.com*.

If you want to pursue representing investors and making that your niche, start by reading through other investors' Web sites, reading books on real estate investing to understand the mind-set of the investor, and reading through news groups and blogs with a high level of investor participation. Ask questions and prepare yourself for what is essentially a new career, a quite lucrative one at that. You may even find a house or two for yourself to buy and begin your own nest egg, which will only make you that much more sensitive to what your clients look for. You may choose to take licensing courses on real estate investing and truly understand this fascinating marketplace.

A9 (2006).
http://maps.a9.com

AOL.
www.aol.com

a la mode, inc. (2006).
About the Company. *www.alamode.com/Default.aspx*

Bankrate (2005).
www.bankrate.com

Bloomberg News (2005).
"Investors Bet on New Homes," April 2005.

Blue Nile Inc. (2005).

Borrell Asssociates Inc. (2005).

Burge, H. (2003).
Cheap Flights Group.

BusinessWeek (April 2005).
"Real Estate's Turf War Heats Up—How Old Line Agents Are Undermining Advances by Online Discount Brokers."

BusinessWeek (May 2004). "The Internet Has Rewritten the Rules for Books, Music and Travel. Which Industries Are Next?"

Caliper Corporation (2006).
www.caliper.com/Maptitude/RealEstate/default.htm

comScore (2005).

Crowston, K., S. Sawyer, and R. Wigand (2001).
"Investigating the interplay between structure and technology in the real estate industry," *Information, Technology and People 14*(2), 163–83.

Crowston, K., and R. Wigand (1999).
"Real estate war in cyberspace: An emerging electronic mar-

ket?" *International Journal of Electronic Markets* 9(1–2), 1–8. (PDF) *http://crowston.syr.edu/real-estate/empaper.pdf*

Crowston, K., S. Sawyer, and R. Wigand. (2004).
"Towards Friction-Free Work: A Multi-Method Study of the Use of Information Technology in the Real-Estate Industry." *http://crowston.syr.edu/real-estate/*

Domania (2006).
www.domania.com

Dugger, M. (2006) Email Interview.
RealtyBaron.com

eHow (2006).
www.ehow.com/how_703_shop-house-online.html

e-Neighborhoods (2006).
www.neighborhoods.com

eNeighborhoods (2005, 2006).
"Raising your Neighborhood IQ." A White Paper Special Report by eNeighborhoods.

e-PRONAR (2006).
FAQs, Course Preview, About e-PRO. Retrieved from the Internet at *www.e-PROnar.com*

ESRI (2006).
http://www.esri.com

Evans (2005).
"New Report Shows Internet Eroding Newspaper Real Estate Advertising."

Fannie Mae (2004).
Economic Data.

Fickes, M. (2003).
"A Technology Lull, You Say?" *National Real Estate Investor,* April 1, 2003. *www.nreionline.com/stategies/technology/real_estate_technology_lull_say/*

Finley, M. (2005).
California State University Northridge. "Community Information by Zip Code." *http://library.csun.edu/mfinley/zipstats.html*

ForSaleByOwner.com.
www.forsalebyowner.com

GIS Development (2006).
"Real Estate technology companies form partnership to expand service." *www.gisdevelopment.net/news/viewn.asp?id=GIS:N_ vzwuihftmx &cat=Business%20News&sub=Merger%20&%20Alliance*

Gartner Group (2004 and 2005).
Gartner Reports.

Gassman, K. (2005).
Rapaport. New York, NY.

Glink, I. (2006).
"What Is the Future of Real Estate in America? Mortgage Bankers Association, the Past and Future of Real Estate in America." October 20, 2005. *www.thinkglink.com/article.asp?Title=The_Past_And_ Future_Of_Real_Estate_ In_America.htm&ID=140*

GURU Networks (2006).
Retrieved from the Internet at *www.gurunet.net*

Guttentag, J. Yahoo Finance.
http://loan.yahoo.com/m/cq_mtgbroker.html

Guttentag, J. Yahoo Finance.
www.mtgprofessor.com/

Guttentag, J. Yahoo Finance.
http://loan.yahoo.com/m/cq_refer.html

Haddad, A. (2005).
"Low-Priced Brokerage Is Shaking up Real Estate," *Los Angeles Times,* December 1, 2005.

Hale, B. (1999)
"Internet Is Transforming Residential Real Estate Industry," *Intercom Online,* November 18, 1999.

HomeGain (2000).
Press Release, October 2000.

HomePriceCheck (2006).
www.homepricecheck.com

HomeSeekers (2006).
www.homeseekers.com

JupiterResearch (2005).
ZDNet Research. *www.zdnet.com*

Kane (2002).
   "Online Travel Bookings on the Rise," CNET News.com.

Klein, S. (2006)
   "NAR's e-PRO: Online Technology Training and Certification." A
   White Paper Special Report by Saul Klein of Internet Crusade.

LendingTree (2005).
   www.lendingtree.com

Levinson, M. (2005).
   "A Season on the Brink," *CIO*, December 1, 2005.

Los Gatos Weekly Times (2005).
   October 12, 2005.

Media Matrix (2004).
   July.

Melanson, W. (2006)
   PropertyGuys Email Interview.

MelissaData (2006).
   www.melissadata.com/Lookups/

Microsoft (2006). Microsoft Case Studies for Real Estate.
   *http://members.microsoft.com/CustomerEvidence/Search/Advanced
   SearchResults.aspx?Flag=0&AndTaxID=25185&AndTaxID=3282*

MIT Center for Real Estate (2006).
   Working Papers and Thesis Papers available at *web.mit.edu/cre*

Mortgage Industry Standards Maintenance Organization (2006).
   www.mismo.org/default.html

Most Home Technologies Corporation (2006).
   Retrieved from the Internet at *www.mosthome.com/overview.html*

National Association of Realtors®.
   www.realtor.org

National Multi Housing Council. (2003).
   Quick Facts: Resident Demographics. Retrieved from the Internet on
   May 25, 2006 at *www.nmhc.org/Content/ServeContent.cfm?Content
   ItemID=1152&IsAdmin=true#characteristics* and *www.nmhc.org/Content/
   ServeContent.cfm?IssueID=253&Content ItemID=150&siteArea=Resources*

Nielsen//NetRatings (2005).
   Ratings Research.

"Online Real Estate Advertising Comes of Age"
Suburban newspaper report.

PhoCusWright (2005).
Online Travel Overview.

PropertyGuys (2006).
Retrieved from the Internet at *www.propertyguys.com*

Real Estate Journal (2006).
Powered by Terraxsite at *www.terraxsite.com/wsj/index.cfm?page=residential*

Real Estate Journal HomePriceCheck (2006).
http://realestatejournal.domania.com/homepricecheck/index.jsp

Real Estate Transaction Standard (2006).
About RETS. *www.rets.org*

RE/MAX.
"RE/MAX Revolutionizes On-Line Real Estate Listing Searches. Historic Changes in Real Estate Industry Helps Consumers Find Homes for Sale." April 13, PRNewswire. *www.remax.com*

REALTOR.com.
www.REALTOR.com

REALTOR.com (2006).
Corporate News and Information. *www.homestore.com/Company/CorporateInfo.asp?lnksrc=RDC-NAV-0006&poe=realtor&gate=realtor*

RealtyTimes (1998).
Retrieved from the Internet on May 25, 2006 at *http://realtytimes.com/rtcpages/19980115_apartment.htm*

Saranow, J. (2002).
The Wall Street Journal Online. May 13, 2002. Tech Q&A–Craigslist Begins to Make a Dent in New York Apartment Market." Retrieved from the Internet on May 25, 2006 at *www.craigslist.org/about/press/nyaptmkt.html*

Sawyer, S., K. Crowston, M. Allbritton, and R. Wigand (2000). "How do information and communication technologies reshape work? Evidence from the residential real estate industry" [Research in progress]. In *Proceedings of the International Conference on Information Systems*, Brisbane, Australia, December 10–13.

Sichelman, L. (2005)
"Lenders Crack Down on Mortgage Fraud," *Los Angeles Times,* December 4. *www.latimes.com/business/la-relew4dec04,1,733443 .story?ctrack=1&cset=true*

Siegel, S. (2006).
eNeighborhoods, Inc. Personal Interview by Email.

Stewart Realty Solutions (2006).
SureClose product; information available at *www.sureclose.com/*

Streitfeld, D. (2005).
"Real Estate Fraud Booms," *Los Angeles Times,* December 5. *www.latimes.com/news/printedition/la-fifraud5dec05,1,6234200 .story?ctrack=1&cset=true*

Sullivan, P. (2006).
Email Interview. GURUNet.net

U.S. Census Bureau.
Households and Famlies 2004 Survey. Retrieved from the Internet on May 25, 2006 at *http://factfinder.census.gov/servlet/STTable?_bm=y&-qr_name=ACS_2004_EST_G00_S1101&-ds _name=ACS_2004_EST_G00_*

ValueYourHome (2006).
http://valueyourhome.realestatejournal.com

VaultWare. (2006).
Retrieved from the Internet on May 25, 2006 at *www.vault ware.com*

Whitehouse (2004).
Real Estate Journal.

Yahoo Finance (2006).
Mortgage Center at *http://finance.yahoo.com/loan/mortgage*

Zamani, P. (2005).
CEO of Next Phase.

Zillow (2006).
www.zillow.com/corp/About.z

ZipRealty (2005).
www.ziprealty.com